The Coaching Shift

The Coaching Shift: How A Coaching Mindset and Skills Can Change You, Your Interactions, and the World Around You offers practical guidance on how to adopt a coaching mindset and how to build a coaching skill set to unlock better communication, stronger relationships, and high performance in others.

Accessible and practical, the book draws on research from coaching, neuroscience, cognitive psychology, social psychology, and industrial-organizational psychology to provide the best science-based practices that can be applied in work and life. It presents core coaching skills that anyone can develop and use to improve their own emotions, thoughts, behaviors, and interactions with others. It uses levels of analysis to help readers think about key concepts first in relation to themselves, then in 1:1 interactions, group and team dynamics, organizational-level impact, and beyond. The book offers specific and tangible advice for readers to develop their coaching and communication skills while also developing a deeper understanding of themselves.

The Coaching Shift, with its clear tone, anecdotal references, and practical application, will be essential reading for coaches in practice and in training, and for academics and students of coaching and coaching psychology. These concepts and practices are also relevant for anyone who wants to have more effective interactions with others.

Shonna D. Waters, PhD, is an organizational psychologist, technologist, leadership coach, and part-time professor at Georgetown University, USA. She spent her career conducting research and consulting on people and organizational systems. She is an executive at BetterUp, where she works to scale human transformation. Shonna also authored *The Practical Guide to HR Analytics*.

Brodie Gregory Riordan, PhD, is an industrial psychologist, executive coach, and part-time professor at Georgetown University, USA. Her career includes global leadership roles at Procter & Gamble, CEB, and McKinsey & Company. She manages Ocular, a coaching and consulting practice based in Washington, DC, and is an executive coach with The Boda Group. Brodie also authored *Feedback Fundamentals and Evidence-Based Best Practices*.

"Shonna D. Waters & Brodie Gregory Riordan have done an extraordinary job of capturing the tools, techniques, and fundamentals needed to successfully build out impactful coaching skills. Their content is deeply pragmatic; through stories, examples, and reflection exercises Coaching Skills empowers readers to unlock one's potential to show up as more curious, present, engaged, and supportive with others. This is a must-read book for anyone who wants to up-level their ability to manage in an organization, lead a team, engage a business partner, or navigate a relationship."

Dr. Jacinta M. Jiménez, PsyD, BCC, Author of *The Burnout Fix* and Vice President, Coach Innovation, BetterUp.

"The best leaders I have worked with, whether within the 75th Ranger Regiment, the world of entrepreneurship, or within McKinsey and Company, Waters and Riordan were the best coaches. These leaders have the self awareness to know that is it more fun and rewarding once we shift from needing to have all the answers, and instead focus on much more effective and scalable ways we can coach ourseves and others - this book gives you the tools you need to achieve this."

Neil Markey, *Co-Founder and CEO of Beckley Retreats*

"With the autonomy of hybrid work comes the opportunity and challenge to take greater command of our own paths to full potential and to process relationships differently. 'Coaching Skills' wisely pivots the focus from coaching up others to coaching up ourselves first. It provides a fresh approach to self-reflection and self-actualization that can unlock new levels of success and well being. And spoiler alert: By strengthening the skills to coach myself, I feel emboldened to facilitate a similar journey in others in a more authentic way. And hasn't that always been the holy grail of coaching from the start? Brilliant move by authors, Waters and Riordan, to know better than to just teach us *how to coach others*."

Joe Fernandez, *SVP of Global Sales at OnFrontiers*

"If you're looking to understand the why and the how through real examples and coaching tools you can put in practice for you or your team this a must read. The Coaching Shift provides the unique combination of teaching the "what" of coaching through concepts and theories AND the "how" of coaching through relatable stories and tools that help you learn more about coaching yourself, team or others from the first chapter through the last chapter. This book lays the platform for continual growth in way that you not only learn how coaching leads to growth but in a way that you can start enacting changes as soon as you complete the first chapter. Waters and

Riordan uniquely explains concepts, with stories, and templates for growth to help the reader learn, and support learning of others."

Kimberly Corbitt, *Senior VP, People & Culture at Phoenix Suns/Phoenix Mercury*

"I thought I knew what it meant to be a great coach – then I read Coaching Skills and it changed everything. Dr. Waters and Dr. Riordan take you on an artful and science-based journey to explore your own life and relationships and share simple and easy ways to use Coaching Skills as a leader, teammate, partner and friend. I recommend this book to anyone looking to improve their life and those around them."

Andrew Biga, *Chief People Officer at GoHealth Urgent Care*

The Coaching Shift

How A Coaching Mindset and Skills Can
Change You, Your Interactions, and the
World Around You

Shonna D. Waters and
Brodie Gregory Riordan

NEW YORK AND LONDON

Cover image: Getty

First published 2023
by Routledge
605 Third Avenue, New York, NY 10158

and by Routledge
4 Park Square, Milton Park, Abingdon, Oxon, OX14 4RN

Routledge is an imprint of the Taylor & Francis Group, an informa business

© 2023 Shonna D. Waters and Brodie Gregory Riordan

Library of Congress Cataloging-in-Publication Data
A catalog record for this book has been requested

ISBN: 978-0-367-76440-1 (hbk)
ISBN: 978-0-367-76439-5 (pbk)
ISBN: 978-1-003-16691-7 (ebk)

DOI: 10.4324/9781003166917

Typeset in Goudy
by Apex CoVantage, LLC

This book was inspired by our students at Georgetown University. Each year we have the privilege of witnessing their growth and self-discovery in our class: Coaching Skills for HR Professionals. Each year we are delighted when students share success stories in which they used their coaching skills not only at work, but in their personal lives, to shift mindsets, unlock possibilities, expand understanding, strengthen relationships, and more. Many have continued to reach out – even years later – to tell us the impact the content made on them and ways they have shared it with others around them. Hearing these stories has been incredibly meaningful for us and left us wanting for other vehicles to extend that impact even more broadly. We believe that adopting a coaching mindset and developing and using coaching skills can help every person better understand themselves and engage more effectively with other people in all domains of their life.

Writing this book was a rewarding partnership for the two of us and would not have been possible without the help of many other wonderful people. Thank you to Ali, Chad, Fred, Yolanda, Lisa, Helen, Ted, Lane, Anna, and Tim for reading early drafts and giving us valuable feedback. Thank you to Montana for being our formatting wizard. Thank you, Taylor for your beautiful and brilliant artistic contributions to the book. Thank you, Angela, James, Ali, and Rose for lending your wisdom and experience to our "spotlights." Thank you to the Georgetown University School of Continuing Studies Coaching program faculty, staff, and fellow students who deepened each of our own coaching journeys and to our mentors who helped us to find our ways there to begin with. Thank you to BetterUp for your work to democratize access to coaching and research to increase and demonstrate its impact.

Thank you, Christina at Taylor & Francis for taking a chance on us with this book. Thank you to Danielle and Maddie for your patience, support, and expertise. Thank you to the entire editorial team at Taylor & Francis/ Routledge for making this a smooth and fun process. Thank you to the four anonymous reviewers who provided feedback on our proposal that helped us refine our ideas and, hopefully, write a stronger end product.

Finally, thank you to our families. We could not have done this without your constant patience, support, and encouragement.

Contents

1
Your roadmap

Questions we'll answer in this chapter:

1. What is coaching?
2. Why does it matter?
3. Why should I read this book and what can I expect?

Imagine this: We zoom in on a modern, suburban office park, and see Marie. She's 34, intelligent, competent, hard-working . . . and she's very sure of it, too. It's mid-afternoon, and Marie is having a somewhat tense conversation with her boss, who is providing feedback to Marie on a recent meeting they had with colleagues in another department. Marie's boss was dreading this conversation, because – although Marie is a high-performer who does great work – she's a nightmare to give feedback to. Marie doesn't *really* listen; she practices what you might call "reloading." When someone else is talking, Marie is largely focused on what she will say next, carefully crafting a response that shows that she knows more and is cleverer than the other person. During this conversation with her boss, Marie doesn't seek to understand the feedback; she focuses on arguing why it's wrong and correcting her boss's misinformed perceptions about the meeting. She leaves the conversation feeling like she won the debate. Her boss leaves feeling exhausted and exasperated.

Later that day, Marie meets up with some friends for drinks. One of Marie's friends shares a story about a bad date she recently went on. While her other friends are laughing and empathizing with their friend, Marie focuses on providing advice. She can see SO CLEARLY what's wrong with her friend's approach to dating and why she has these horror stories. Her friend patiently listens and thanks Marie for the advice, but thinks to herself, "Yeah, that's not at all what I want. Thank goodness my dating life isn't like Marie's! I would hate the kind of relationships she's been in."

DOI: 10.4324/9781003166917-1

Marie has great intentions. She just wants to be a high performer, see her organization and her team succeed, help her friends find true love, and reassure her boss that everything is under control. But the way that Marie chooses to engage in these important situations, with people who play central roles in her work and life, leaves so much opportunity on the table. The conversations with her boss and her friends were opportunities to learn, grow, and deepen connections. But Marie missed out on all of this value because of her mindset and her behavior. Marie was more interested in being *right* than in seeking to understand the other person's perspective. She was more interested in closing down the conversation and having the last word than in drawing out more information or being curious. Marie prioritized demonstrating her competence and her expertise over connecting meaningfully with someone who was willing to be vulnerable.

By prioritizing being right over learning, growing, and connecting, Marie is missing out on valuable opportunities to connect and have more productive outcomes both for herself and with others. If we could rewind time and give Marie the opportunity to "do-over" both situations, she could have practiced some essential skills like really listening, seeking to understand, asking questions to get more information and draw the other person out, or noticing the tone, emotions, and body language of her boss as he shared feedback or her friend as she discussed her date. Bringing these skills to these conversations would have resulted in very different outcomes for Marie, her boss, and her friend. Marie would have learned and found opportunities to grow and be an even stronger performer. Her boss would have felt heard and confident that Marie would continue to grow. Marie could have learned more about her friend and strengthened their relationship through empathy and listening. Her friend would feel supported and affirmed.

In the chapters that follow we will explore a variety of mindsets, beliefs, emotions, behaviors, and skills. We approach these from the lens of coaching, but at the core these are uniquely human capabilities that are helpful in any human interactions, not just coaching conversations. In Marie's case, she could have used some key coaching skills, like really listening and asking questions, to have more effective conversations. Similarly, her boss could have used a coaching approach to raise Marie's awareness to her mindset in their feedback conversation.

Our goal in this book is to synthesize some of the most important theories, concepts, and approaches we have learned in our training and experiences as coaches, and to present them in a way that is useful both within and outside of a coaching context. You might be surprised to see that we don't really dig in on coaching skills until Chapter 4, but when we do, we try to make it clear that the skills are portable and can be used in just about any conversation, not just a coaching conversation. Our goal is that you take from this book new ways of thinking about yourself and others, as well as some tangible skills that you can use in a coaching conversation and other conversations where you want to show up as more curious, present, engaged, and supportive. Adopting this coaching mindset and skill set will enable you to unlock new ways of thinking about and framing your world, a higher quality of conversation, your own and others' potential, and new ways of connecting with others.

Unlock your potential for connection

Humans evolved to be social creatures because we can accomplish far more together than we can individually.[1] Despite exponentially more technology and automation than we had 50 years ago, people are no less important in our ability to accomplish our goals today. In fact, according to the World Economic Forum's *Future of Jobs Report*,[2] it is the uniquely human skills, such as coordinating with others, emotional intelligence, and cognitive flexibility, that are most critical in the fourth industrial revolution.[3] But working closely with others can also be complicated. Take Marie, for example. Marie missed out on essential opportunities to empathize with and understand important people in her life – including her boss and a good friend. Despite her best intentions of being a supportive friend and a high-performing team member, Marie was so focused on her own need to be right or validated, her own judgments and insecurities, that she completely missed emotional cues and openings to connect with others. Her behavior, in turn, elicited commensurate emotions and assumptions in her boss and her friend. Emotions, assumptions, beliefs, fears, biases, and past experiences color every human interaction in the workplace and beyond. Failure to empathize, listen, and fully understand one another can get in the way of effective collaboration and impact both interpersonal and organizational dynamics.

Our world is increasingly volatile, uncertain, complex, and ambiguous. These conditions have forced a new structure of work and shift in the psychological contract between employees and employers. At work, leaders and individual employees face feelings of instability or anxiety and adapt to shifting priorities as markets and global conditions change rapidly. To keep up with the pace of change, organizational structures and decision making need to be more agile and distributed. During the 2020 global COVID-19 pandemic organizations had to rapidly adapt and innovate or suffer significant setbacks. Nearly overnight, organizations and the leaders and employees within them faced the shift to remote working, dramatic changes in service industries, sudden demand for healthcare and personal protective equipment (PPE) solutions, among other things. Even the most resilient organizations, leaders, and individuals were put to the test as the situation unfolded rapidly, with far-reaching consequences few anticipated.

As an example, the pandemic had a massive impact on the global events industry, which thrives on conferences, conventions, weddings, and more. Prior to COVID-19, the business events sector was larger than consumer electronics and computers, and office equipment. When large gatherings and in-person meet-ups were canceled, postponed, or converted to virtual formats in response to the pandemic, events companies had to quickly pivot in order to survive. For example, SnapBar, a photo booth rental company, had previously been named the fastest growing company of the year by Inc. Magazine. Leaders at SnapBar had to quickly come up with viable and creative solutions to keep their business afloat. Within *four days* they launched "Keep Your City Smiling," which sells gift boxes with products from local small businesses and a healthcare giftbox for frontline workers.[4]

Technical skills serve us well in known situations. But in the face of uncertainty, technical skills aren't enough. Imagine what it took for organizations to shift so quickly. Company leaders had to scan the world around them and make quick decisions about whether to stay the course or whether to put the previously established strategic plan and company goals aside and start anew. Given that no one knew how long the pandemic would last or how extreme the consequences would be, those decisions could not have been easy. They had to first reconcile their own uncertainty, fears, emotions . . . and then they had to lead others. They had to align a workforce around a new mission, purpose, and set of protocols. Together, they had to build a new business – identify a new supply chain, train workers, and plan for an unknown future. This was likely all while adapting to changes in their personal lives. Schools closed, travel stopped, loved ones may have needed care, and personal safety became top of mind during formerly mundane activities, like grocery shopping.

Dealing with our own responses to volatility and uncertainty is challenging enough and can feel even more complicated when we also have to interact with others who bring their own set of beliefs, emotions, fears, assumptions, and biases. Managing our thoughts and emotions as we navigate a rapidly evolving workplace and world is challenging and can feel downright overwhelming when we layer on complex interpersonal dynamics. As trained coaches, psychologists, and professors of coaching, we have come to discover

over the years that coaching skills can make interacting with others easier, and are valuable no matter your role, tenure, or industry.

How this connects to coaching

Since you picked up this book you probably already have some sense of what coaching is. Perhaps you have worked with a coach at some point in your life – though it may have been to improve your performance on the field rather than in the office. In our work, we find that many people have a misconception that coaching requires expertise and advice-giving, when in fact, it's very much the opposite. Professional coaches "partner with clients in a thought-provoking and creative process that inspires them to maximize their personal and professional potential."[5] One of our favorite metaphors for coaching is teaching someone to fish, which will feed them for a lifetime, rather than giving them a fish, which will feed them for only a day. If you, too, have the misconception that coaching is sharing advice and imparting your wisdom on the person you are coaching, each coaching conversation would be the equivalent of giving that person a single fish. They may leave with an answer (and a full belly) but have not learned or grown in the process. When you shift your understanding of coaching to a belief in the value of that person solving their own problems, coming to their own solutions, and developing their skills along the way, you are helping them learn to fish and have food for a lifetime.

Coaches help others learn rather than telling them what to do. This is important, because just like your soccer coach won't be able to talk you through every move during the championship game, your professional coach can't run the plays in your big meeting. You must be able to solve problems on your own. If it's advice and direction you are looking for, a mentor, manager, or other trusted advisor will serve you better than a coach. Given the uncertainty, volatility, and change that we're experiencing, you're likely to encounter challenges that no one has encountered before. If you want to chart your own path, or a path through uncharted territory, you likely need to find the answers within. That is where coaching comes in.

Why coaching?

You might be asking yourself what makes coaching so special? Professional coaching emerged as a subdiscipline of consulting between the 1950s and 1970s, in conjunction with the formalization of other leadership development initiatives in organizations such as development programs and multi-rater feedback. By the 1980s, many consulting companies had developed coaching services and research began. Today, evidence suggests that coaching is a highly effective intervention. One possible reason coaching is so effective is because it is inherently aligned with many of the most enduring findings in psychology and behavioral science more broadly.[6] As an example, return to our metaphor of giving a man a fish versus teaching him to fish so that he can eat forever. If the man can show up every day and get his meal handed to him, does it matter that he doesn't know how to fish for himself? Psychological research would say yes. People value agency – a feeling of control over actions and their consequences – and are more bought into things they choose for themselves.[7] This means that although the man's appetite might be satiated by being given a fish each day, he will be more satisfied with the meal if he caught it himself. The mindsets, behaviors, and practices that have come to be bundled under the label of coaching provide a potent and convenient bundle of tools that can be used together in formal coaching conversations or developed and applied across situations.

Coaching is like teaching someone to fish

Coaching can take many forms. Professional coaches may work with or for organizations to coach leaders and individuals on their careers, in support of their development, or to help them navigate personal transitions. Coaching is often infused into development-oriented performance management processes, talent initiatives such as learning and development, high-potential programs or succession management, and even to help employees who are exiting an organization figure out their next career horizon. Many organizations also invest in developing the coaching skills of leaders or HR managers so they will bring a more coach-like approach to their day-to-day work. **In this book we focus less on the professional practice of coaching or role of a coach, and more on the core coaching skill set that we believe anyone can develop and use to improve their own emotions, thoughts, behaviors, and interactions with others.** In an article for The Institute of Coaching, researcher John Campbell notes that a coaching approach can "be used in any situation where someone wants something to be different" and help another person figure out what they really want, learn from an experience, become more self-aware, get a level of support or healthy challenge that they may not get from other conversations, among many other things.[8] In other words, adopting a coaching approach can help create a *shift* in yourself, others, or in situations.

> In this book we focus less on the professional practice of coaching or role of a coach, and more on the core coaching skill set that we believe anyone can develop and use to improve their own emotions, thoughts, behaviors, and interactions with others.

As an industry, professional coaching has exploded over the last 40 years, largely because of the array of positive outcomes linked to working with a coach. The International Coaching Federation estimates that the number of leadership coach practitioners increased by 33% globally between 2015 and 2019, and the number of leaders using coaches rose by 46%.[9] Coaching enhances performance, well-being, the ability to cope with change, work attitudes such as job satisfaction and engagement,[10] skill development,[11] clarity and goal attainment.[12] It is among the most effective interventions to build resilience.[13] Coaching has even been shown to boost both team performance[14] and organizational performance.[15]

With results like those, it's no wonder that organizations are training managers to incorporate coaching skills into their leadership style. A study conducted in 2018 by the Human Capital Institute and International Coaching Federation found that a third of companies are investing in such training for their managers.[16] Employees whose managers are skilled at development have higher performance, are more committed to their organization, and are 40% more likely to stay with the company.[17] As Ibarra and Scoular[18] note in their *Harvard Business Review* article "The Leader as Coach," a leader who brings an effective coaching approach to their interactions with others "asks questions instead of providing answers, supports employees instead of judging them, and facilitates their development instead of dictating what has to be done" (p. 111).

The evidence is compelling that coaching skills can be used to improve the performance and well-being of others. Using a more coach-like approach will help you build more meaningful relationships and have smoother, more effective, and higher impact interactions with others. And yes, it will likely improve your performance and the performance of those around you. **In this book we argue that adopting the mindsets and behaviors necessary to coach others, coach yourself, and be open to coaching can unlock possibilities, opportunities, and connections you may otherwise miss out on.** Effective coaching requires listening, humility, and curiosity. Being a better listener, living with humility, and opening up your curiosity will help you better manage day-to-day interactions with others and will also help you unlock new ways of thinking about, seeing, and being in the world. By embodying a coaching mindset, you will be able to see the people you interact with every day more fully. They will walk away from your conversations feeling seen and heard.

Listening   Curiosity   Humility

And, yes, you read that second one correctly – coaching *yourself*. When we work 1:1 with executive coaching clients, we are not only helping them work through immediate challenges or goals, we are also helping them develop a new inner monologue and way of thinking about and approaching problems, so that ultimately they can self-coach. We think of this as embodying a coaching approach. We believe that the skills, mindsets, and concepts we discuss in this book will help you unlock new ways of thinking about and understanding yourself, new ways of thinking about and relating to others, and new ways of approaching people and situations.

The everyone coach

We did not write this book with professional coaches in mind. In fact, the greatest inspiration for this book is our students – past, present, and future – in the Coaching Skills course we teach in the Georgetown University HR master's degree program. Our students, who cover a wide range of ages, backgrounds, industries, occupations, and life experiences, come into class with preconceived notions about what coaching is and is not. They start the semester with beliefs about who they are, who others are, and how to get the best from others. They all come to class thinking they are good listeners . . . and quickly realize they are not. Few people are. We wrote this book for all the students, teachers, managers, leaders, parents, neighbors, health care professionals, service industry workers, and non-profit volunteers in our lives. If you are a person, and/or you interact with people – this book is for you (how's that for specificity).

Back to Marie

Let's get back to Marie. Imagine you could rewind the tape and see Marie approach the conversations with her boss and her friend with a more coach-like attitude. In this version of the story, rather than focusing on being *right* and convincing her boss that the feedback on the meeting is wrong, Marie instead decides to **listen**. She doesn't just listen to respond, but to really understand. Marie is **curious** about her boss's perspective and wants to understand what went well and what could have been more effective in the meeting – and why it matters. She listens not only with her ears, but also with her eyes – noting her boss's facial expressions and body language, in addition to words and tone. Marie asks open-ended **questions** to learn more, such as: "Thank you for sharing your observations with me. I want our next meeting with this team to be more effective. I know we have a meeting again in two weeks. What's your vision for what "better" looks like in our interactions with this team?" As a result, she leaves the conversation with increased **self-awareness** – including a clearer understanding of what she's doing well in these meetings and what she can try differently next time to have a more productive outcome. She and her boss both feel comfortable and relieved coming out of the conversation – as if they are truly on the same side and working together toward the same goals. The conversation increased feelings of trust between them.

Walking into happy hour with her friends, Marie feels both grounded and motivated. She feels like she is doing good work and has some new behaviors to "try on" in the weeks to come. She draws on the same deep **listening** skills as her friend recalls her recent bad date. Marie finds herself making an assumption about her friend's dating patterns, but stops herself and asks a **curious question** instead. As her friend wraps up her story with a laugh, Marie asks, "Candace, if you were aware you had so little in common with this person, why did you agree to go on a date with them?" Marie has an assumption that Candace is just desperate and going on dates with anyone and everyone. Candace's answer is not at all what Marie expected: "Oh, it was for a charity auction! I donated a date to my favorite non-profit and it raised $1,500!" Marie laughed and realized how quick and wrong her initial judgment had been.

In this "do-over," Marie reaches very different outcomes in both conversations. She **learns from both experiences** and **forges deeper connections** with others. She practices **deep listening** and **seeking to understand** more from others. She learns that her assumptions may not be accurate! She lets go of the pressure to be right and is able to relax and let more in. In this second version of Marie's day, she leverages key coaching skills to have more productive interactions. Coaching draws heavily from psychology, which involves the scientific study of relationships between the brain, environment, and behavior.[19] In this book, you'll be introduced to some foundational principles that will shift how you make sense of your experiences and those of the people around you. We have strong beliefs about the ripple effect that adopting a coaching mindset and applying coaching skills can have for you and those around you. We've structured the book in a way that we hope makes you believe this, too, by the end.

What you'll find in the chapters ahead

In Part 1 (Chapters 2 and 3), we'll focus on **YOU**. More specifically, we'll focus on psychology as a tool to help you better understand your own thoughts, feelings, and behavior. In Chapter 2, you'll learn more about the ways your mind shapes your experience. You'll learn what a **coaching mindset** is and how to adopt one. In Chapter 3, we'll do a deep dive on behavior. We'll explore how thoughts, feelings, and behaviors connect and influence each other. We'll look at the impact of goals and motivation on our behavior. Part 1 is the foundation that will help you be a better coach to yourself and to others. In our experience, doing a little "self work" first is imperative for you to be present and effective when applying your coaching skills with others.

Coaching Skill Set

Coaching Mindset

Coaching Impact

In Part 2, we shift our focus to **your coaching skills,** or toolkit. We'll show you how you can use your deepened awareness of yourself and your understanding of people in general to build stronger relationships and co-ordinate with others more easily. This will require **building coaching skills** on top of the coaching mindset that we laid the foundation for in Part 1. In Chapter 4, you'll *finally* learn about core coaching skills. And in Chapter 5, we'll explore how you can use those skills with groups and teams. As we noted earlier, people can accomplish more with others than they can on their own. Many of our goals don't require the help of just one other person. We work in teams or groups to accomplish our most important and ambitious goals.

In Part 3, we shift to **your coaching impact.** Now that you have taken a closer look at yourself and learned some essential coaching skills, you'll want to think about how you can put those skills to good use. In Chapter 6 we focus on coaching in organizations. We will explore the ways a coaching mindset can help build a culture that fosters human potential and flourishing. In Chapter 7, you'll learn about ways to take your new coaching skills out into the broader world for positive impact and change. A coaching mindset can impact the way you show up in the world more broadly. It can reduce tension around political polarization at your next dinner with your extended family, enable you to make and communicate decisions at work that are met with less resistance, and help you negotiate with less conflict the next time your teenager is asking you for something. Through it all, we'll share the evidence behind the principles but also provide practical tools to practice and reflect so that you can immediately apply the concepts to your life. We'll share cases, stories, research, and examples to illustrate the application of key coaching principles in both work and life settings and relationships. We include reflection questions in each chapter to help you pause, think, and apply the concepts you're reading about to your own experience. Reflection, too, is an essential part of coaching.[20] Pausing to reflect gives you the time and space to really process what you are reading, to crystalize learning, and make sense of your experiences. New to reflection? Now is a great time to start. We encourage you to let go of any self-judgment around your responses to these reflection questions – write in sentences, bullets, stream of consciousness – whatever speaks to you. And if you don't want to write directly in the book, grab a notebook or piece of scrap paper. This reflection is for you and you alone!

Experience if yourself

What inspired you to pick up this book? What are you hoping to get from reading it?

_____

_____

_____

_____

What is your definition of coaching coming into this book? How have you used coaching skills in the past?

_____

_____

_____

How will you apply or experiment with concepts you learn in this book? Reading can be eye-opening and interesting, but to truly change our mindsets and behavior we have to try on some new things! What works best for you when you want to build new skills?

_____

_____

_____

_____

Think of a time when you felt like someone was really listening to you. Not going through the motions but listening with interest and their full attention. What was that experience like for you?

_____

_____

_____

_____

Recall a conversation that didn't go as well as you hoped. How does that experience relate to Marie?

_____

_____

_____

_____

Chapter 1 Key idea

Coaching skills are human skills and can be used by anyone, in any role (including outside of work!). This book will help you develop your coaching mindset and skill set and apply these in your everyday life.

Notes

1 Harari, Y. N. (2014). *Sapiens: A brief history of humankind.* New York, NY: Random House.
2 Young Global Leaders. (2016). *World economic forum annual meeting 2016: Mastering the fourth industrial revolution.* https://www3.weforum.org/docs/Media/AM16/AM16MediaFactSheet.pdf
3 According to Klaus Schwab, Founder and Executive Chairman of the World Economic Forum, the fourth industrial revolution is characterized by the "blurring of boundaries between the physical, digital, and biological worlds."
4 Taylor, S. J. (2020). *How the SnapBar made a creative pivot to help their team and other small businesses.* Workest by Zenefits. www.zenefits.com/workest/seattle-companys-pivot-is-helping-other-businesses-stay-afloat/
5 International Coaching Federation. (2021). *ICF core competencies.* https://coachfederation.org/core-competencies
6 Kraiger, K., & Ford, J. K. (2021). The science of workplace instruction: Learning and development applied to work. *Annual Review of Organizational Psychology and Organizational Behavior,* 8(4), 45–72. https://doi.org/10.1146/annurev-orgpsych-012420-060109
7 Deci, E. L., & Ryan, R. M. (2012). Self-determination theory. In P. A. M. Van Lange, A. W. Kruglanski, & E. T. Higgins (Eds.), *Handbook of theories of social psychology* (pp. 416–436). Sage Publications Ltd. https://doi.org/10.4135/9781446249215.n21
8 Campbell, J. (2017). *Coaching and 'coaching approach': What's the difference?* The Institute of Coaching. https://instituteofcoaching.org/blogs/coaching-and-coaching-approach-whats-difference

9 International Coaching Federation. (2020). *ICF global coaching study*. https:// coachfederation.org/app/uploads/2020/09/FINAL_ICF_GCS2020_Executive Summary.pdf

10 Jones, R. J., Woods, S. A., & Guillaume, Y. R. (2016). The effectiveness of workplace coaching: A meta-analysis of learning and performance outcomes from coaching. *Journal of Occupational and Organizational Psychology*, 89(2), 249–277. https://doi.org/10.1111/joop.12119

11 Theeboom, T., Beersma, B., & van Vianen, A. E. (2014). Does coaching work? A meta-analysis on the effects of coaching on individual level outcomes in an organizational context. *The Journal of Positive Psychology*, 9(1), 1–18. https://doi.org/10.1080/17439760.2013.837499

12 Grant, A. M., Curtayne, L., & Burton, G. (2009). Executive coaching enhances goal attainment, resilience and workplace well-being: A randomised controlled study. *The Journal of Positive Psychology*, 4(5), 396–407. https://doi.org/10.1080/17439760902992456

   Mosteo, L. P., Batista-Foguet, J. M., Mckeever, J. D., & Serlavós, R. (2016). Understanding cognitive-emotional processing through a coaching process: The influence of coaching on vision, goal-directed energy, and resilience. *The Journal of Applied Behavioral Science*, 52(1), 64–96. https://doi.org/10.1177/0021886315600070

13 Vanhove, A. J., Herian, M. N., Perez, A. L., Harms, P. D., & Lester, P. B. (2016). Can resilience be developed at work? A meta-analytic review of resilience-building programme effectiveness. *Journal of Occupational and Organizational Psychology*, 89(2), 278–307. https://doi.org/10.1111/joop.12123

14 Grant, A. M. (2006). A personal perspective on professional coaching and the development of coaching psychology. *International Coaching Psychology Review*, 1(1), 12–22.

   Kampa-Kokesch, S., & Anderson, M. Z. (2001). Executive coaching: A comprehensive review of the literature. *Consulting Psychology Journal: Practice and Research*, 53(4), 205–228. https://doi.org/10.1037/1061-4087.53.4.205

   Peterson, D. B. (1996). Executive coaching at work: The art of one-on-one change. *Consulting Psychology Journal: Practice and Research*, 48(2), 78–86. https://doi.org/10.1037/1061-4087.48.2.78

15 Evered, R. D., & Selman, J. C. (1989). Coaching and the art of management. *Organizational Dynamics*, 18(2), 16–32. https://doi.org/10.1016/0090-2616(89)90040-5

   Fourines, F. F. (1987). *Coaching for improved work performance*. New York: McGraw-Hill, Liberty Hall Press.

   Orth, C. D., Wilkinson, H. E., & Benfari, R. C. (1987). The manager's role as coach and mentor. *Organizational Dynamics*, 15(4), 66–74. https://doi.org/10.1016/0090-2616(87)90045-3

   Popper, M., & Lipshitz, R. (1992). Coaching on leadership. *Leadership & Organization Development Journal*, 13(7), 15–18. https://doi.org/10.1108/01437739210022865

16 Filipkowski, J., Ruth, M., & Heverin, A. (2018). *Building a coaching culture for change management*. Human Capital Institute and International Coaching Federation.

https://academy.webvent.tv/uploads/assets/264/document/BuildingACoaching
CultureForCM_2018.pdf

17 Corporate Leadership Council. (2004). *Driving performance and retention through employee engagement.* Washington, DC: Corporate Executive Board. www.st cloudstate.edu/humanresources/_files/documents/supv-brown-bag/employee-en gagement.pdf

18 Ibarra, H., & Scoular, A. (2019, November–December). The leader as coach. *Harvard Business Review.* https://hbr.org/2019/11/the-leader-as-coach

19 American Psychological Association. (2022). *About APA: Definition of psychology.* www.apa.org/about Grant. (2006). Professional coaching, 12–22.

20 Porter, J. (2017, March 21). Why you should make time for reflection (even if you hate doing it). *Harvard Business Review.* https://hbr.org/2017/03/why-you-should-make-time-for-self-reflection-even-if-you-hate-doing-it

Part 1

You

Ready to do a deep dive into yourself? In Part 1 we'll explore your thoughts, feelings, and actions. In Chapter 2, we focus on your efficient brain – including the mental shortcuts that influence how you perceive the world around you and process information, as well as your emotions. We'll explore the concept of mindset and some strategies that you can use to be more aware of what you are experiencing. In Chapter 3, we focus on behavior, including goals, motivation, and the relationship between thoughts, feelings, and behavior. Our intention in Part 1 is to help you better understand your own thoughts, feelings, and behavior so that you can help others do the same when you start practicing your coaching skills with them. After all, it's hard to help others do something that we haven't yet mastered ourselves! As we mentioned in Chapter 1, this "self work" lays an important foundation for you to be present, aware, and better able to choose how you want to show up in your interactions with others. Don't worry – we'll get to coaching mindset and skills soon.

DOI: 10.4324/9781003166917-2

2
Your efficient brain

Questions we'll answer in this chapter:

1. How do we process information and what impacts how we respond?
2. What can go wrong?
3. How does this relate to coaching?

Tanielle was a successful account manager. After college, she climbed the ranks in her organization quickly and was now leading a team. One day at work, her manager announced that one of her peers was being promoted and moving into another role. As she discussed it with her partner over dinner, she felt herself getting upset. Her partner, trying to show support, noted that Tanielle was far more qualified and a much harder worker. She clearly wasn't appreciated, and it might be time to move on. Tanielle had been happy at work but found herself *noticing* things now. Her manager didn't recognize her publicly when her team exceeded their goals last quarter. She started replaying past conversations and situations back through her mind, interpreting them in a new way. She was feeling overlooked and like she wasn't getting the recognition and opportunities for advancement she thought she deserved. She started to feel undervalued, unappreciated, and a strong sense of resentment. Those feelings motivated her to *behave* differently. She started looking for other jobs.

Tanielle ultimately decided to submit her resignation. Her manager expressed genuine surprise. Tanielle shared that she was looking for more recognition and career growth. Her manager was apologetic, but also adamant that she didn't realize that Tanielle was interested in a new challenge. She had always seen her as one of their rising stars. Her manager expressed regret that they missed the opportunity to help her find what she was looking for internally.

How did Tanielle go from happy to resentful? We are surrounded by data. At any given moment, your brain is trying to make sense of what you see, hear,

DOI: 10.4324/9781003166917-3

taste, and feel in the outside world and in your own inner world. And there are many ways to interpret those data . . .

Experience it yourself

Call to mind a challenge or frustrating situation you are currently navigating. This could be personal or work-related. In this exercise you will reflect on your experience of the situation, and then adopt an alternative perspective to try and see the situation from another person's viewpoint. Grab a pen or pencil and take 5–10 minutes to explore the situation.

Start with your own perspective.

Describe the situation at a high level.

_____

_____

_____

_____

What do you find frustrating, challenging, or unfair about the situation?

_____

_____

_____

_____

What do you know or believe to be true about the situation, your role, and other people involved in that situation?

_____

_____

_____

_____

What is your ideal outcome or resolution for the situation?

_____

_____

_____

_____

Now, adopt the perspective of another person who is involved in this situation.

How would that person describe the situation?

_____

_____

_____

_____

What might they find frustrating or challenging about the situation?

_____

_____

_____

_____

What might they know about the situation that you do not?

_____

_____

_____

_____

What do you know about the situation that THEY do not?

_____

_____

_____

_____

What do you think their ideal outcome or resolution is?

_____

_____

_____

_____

Now, compare the two perspectives

Where do you and the other person have similar perspectives, beliefs, or goals regarding the situation?

_____

_____

_____

_____

Where do your perspectives, beliefs, or goals differ?

_____

_____

_____

_____

How might you explain those differences?

_____

_____

_____

_____

Reflect on the exercise. If you were going to write a "bumper sticker" version of your takeaway, what would it say? For example: "We are both the narrator and the hero in our own story."

_____

_____

_____

_____

Nosce te ipsum (know thyself)

All day, every day, we are inundated with stimuli and information. Some studies estimate that on any given day we are bombarded with as much as 34 gigabytes worth of information.[1] To put that in perspective, if your iPhone has 64 GB of storage, this is the equivalent to processing roughly 50% of everything on your iPhone – apps, music, photos, emails, texts – every single day, and often in new and novel situations. Studies have shown that our brains can process between two and sixty bits of information per second.[2] Most of this processing – including sensations and perception – occurs outside of our conscious awareness. Our brains are equipped with automatic processes and strategies for sorting and filtering through that information. In other words, our brains are outrageously efficient.

As a result, our brains can also be lazy and get us into trouble. Our brains rely on heuristics, shortcuts, and biases to help us operate in the world. The upside of this is that we can quickly make decisions and navigate the world around us. The downside is that we don't always think deeply about everything we are doing. Understanding what is happening in your brain and what drives your own behavior and choices is imperative to being able to work more effectively with other people. Recognizing the biases and limitations of our own thought processes can help us to be more intentional about how we process information in the situations we face day-to-day to be more open, fair, and balanced in how we interpret and perceive others' behaviors.

You might be thinking, "Isn't this supposed to be a book about coaching skills? Why are we talking about the brain?" Working and interacting more effectively with others (such as through the use of your coaching skills) requires us to first understand ourselves and how we make sense of the world. Being aware of and recognizing the fast, automatic processes in our judgment, perception, and decision making enables us to work with that wiring; to make deliberate choices about when and where we want to pause and engage in more effortful thinking.

In our class on coaching skills at Georgetown University, our students learn about their own biases and the way their brains work before diving into key coaching skills. In this chapter, we will cover some of our favorite research from psychology and neuroscience to help you, our reader, deepen your understanding of what is happening in your brain everyday as you judge, perceive, and interpret the world around you (and, most complex of all, others' behavior!). Your emotions and cognition drive how you see and experience the world, how you interpret and make sense of your experiences. Emotions are faster and stronger. Rational thought takes time to catch up – an important distinction we'll talk more about. Your emotions and cognitions jointly inform your behavior – sometimes in ways that are automatic (stimulus-response; reacting) and sometimes in slower and more deliberate ways (cognition). You always have a choice in how you respond. The purpose of this chapter is to explore these two systems, how they impact your behavior, and tools and strategies that you can use to make more deliberate choices to change your behavior and break a stimulus-response cycle.

Cognition: Heuristics, shortcuts, and biases, oh my!

What is the probability that you will be involved in a commercial plane crash? In reality, the likelihood is somewhere between one in 5.4 million and one in 11 million.[3] But if you make a habit of reading or watching the news, you may believe that likelihood to be much higher. If you ever took a social psychology class, you may have learned about the **availability heuristic**.[4] The availability heuristic is our tendency to overestimate how likely or common something is simply because we hear about it more often and are able to easily recall examples. Cable news shows get much better viewership by sharing the breaking news about a plane crash than they ever would by highlighting the thousands of successful commercial flights that take off and land at their destination every single day. The same can be said about the frequency of shark attacks, child abductions, and winning lottery ticket purchases. Other natural human biases, like negativity bias, which is our tendency to pay more attention to negative events and information than to positive or neutral events and information, also feed into what is showcased in the news cycle.

The availability heuristic is one example of the shortcuts and biases our efficient brain relies on to quickly make judgments and decisions based on the information that is readily available to us.[5] These shortcuts are adaptive and important. They enable us to quickly process information or make decisions based on limited information. These shortcuts rely on past experiences and patterns – what we've seen previously or has worked for us in the past. Unfortunately, these quick judgements and reliance on patterns and past experiences result in cognitive biases. We may ignore information that is not consistent with our beliefs, or we may make poor choices as a result of jumping to conclusions or not considering the uniqueness or nuance of the present situation.

In his book, *Thinking Fast and Slow*, Nobel prize winning psychologist Daniel Kahneman[6] describes two systems of thinking: System 1 and System 2. Biases, shortcuts, and heuristics are part of Kahneman's System 1: fast, automatic processing and intuition. On the other hand, when we pause to think deeply and deliberately about something we are engaging System 2. System 2 thinking requires mental energy and effort. Examples of System 1 thinking include brushing your teeth for the 10,000th time in your life or cooking a dinner recipe that you have made time and again, driving your car to work following the same route you have followed for the last 5 years. All of these are effortless and automatic. You reserve your cognitive resources for more complex, novel tasks that will require more deliberate thought. The downside is that you make assumptions, you miss details and nuances, you may not be fully present in what you are doing. On the other hand, engaging in System 2 thinking requires your full presence of mind, your full attention, and significant effort and cognitive resources. Examples of System 2 thinking include test driving a new car on a new road you've never driven before, doing a complex math problem, looking carefully for your friend in a crowded concert.

Stereotypes are another example of cognitive biases and shortcuts. Stereotypes arise from frequently associating one thing with another, then applying that association to future experiences. We often talk about stereotypes in the context of race, gender, or culture. We apply stereotypes to groups of people based on assumptions and associations we have about them. The problem is that all individuals are unique and different. When we apply a stereotype of a group to an individual, we fail to understand who that person is as a unique individual. Pause for a moment to think about some stereotypes you hold. We'll help you.

Experience it yourself

What is one stereotype you hold about a group of people?
Note – stereotypes can be positive too!

_____

_____

_____

_____

Where did that stereotype originate for you?

_____

_____

_____

_____

Now, think of an individual you know who is part of that group. Does
the stereotype you hold apply to that person?

_____

_____

_____

_____

You are likely building awareness for how wrong the stereotypes we form about others can be. Now reflect on how this applies to stereotypes that others have of you, or that you might have of yourself. Follow the format, "I AM . . . BUT I AM NOT . . ." (e.g., "I am *a mother*, but I am not *the primary caretaker*" "I am *sensitive*, but I am not *weak*")

I AM _____ BUT I AM NOT _____

I AM _____ BUT I AM NOT _____

I AM _____ BUT I AM NOT _____

I AM _____ BUT I AM NOT _____

I AM _____ BUT I AM NOT _____

How does labeling something help us in our day-to-day lives? How might it hold us back?

_____

_____

_____

_____

The stereotypes we hold can quickly become expectations we have for people. These expectations, in turn, can influence how we behave and interact with them. For example, if you have a belief that people from New York are aggressive, you may act in a way that provokes aggressive behavior from them. This is known as a *self-fulfilling prophecy* or Pygmalion effect.[7] You may also engage in another bias known as **confirmation bias.**[8] If you believe people from New York are aggressive, you will be more attuned to the aggressive behaviors they exhibit and may unintentionally ignore or fail to notice friendly, calm, or passive behaviors. When we engage in confirmation bias, we are looking for information that reinforces our beliefs and expectations. We are often unaware that we are doing this. Our brains are working to protect our egos all on their own. If you're looking for examples of confirmation bias, look no further than your social media feed. Most people surround themselves with people and information that confirm and support their beliefs. As much as we dread writing this, politics in the United States is a great example! You think COVID-19 is a hoax? You probably prefer news articles that support that belief. You think climate change is real? You will gravitate toward news articles that provide evidence of the reality and gravity of climate change.

Once more, you might be asking yourself: *what does this have to do with coaching?* Learning about how your brain works is like stretching before a big workout. We want you to be able to recognize *how* you think, make judgments, and make sense of situations. Noticing and self-awareness are essential behaviors in coaching. Using a coaching approach can help others become more self-aware and notice more about their experiences, reactions, thoughts, and patterns. To bring our best selves to coaching conversations, we must also deepen our self-awareness and practice noticing in ourselves and others. Becoming aware of your own biases and the lenses that color your perception will help you more effectively coach others, and generally have more effective interactions with them.

You might be thinking, "Wow, I am just cruising through life on autopilot. My brain is making these fast, automatic judgments and I'm asleep at the wheel most of the time." Yes, there is some truth to that. AND **you have more choice than you realize.** Our brains are amazing, fine-tuned information-processing machines. If we paid deep, deliberate attention to every experience, decision, or input we encountered every day, we would break down in a state of complete overwhelm. Our brain's automatic processing frees up our cognitive space and enables us to choose the people, experiences, and decisions where we want to devote focused, deliberate attention. What we want you to take away here is: You can choose where and when you want to switch on that deliberate attention and spend your cognitive resources.

Coaching has two roles to play here. One is that noticing these patterns in ourselves and others and making more conscious choices (i.e., overriding system 1 thinking with system 2) can help us build a stronger muscle and get more comfortable making deliberate choices in the future. The other is that although we can effectively build our awareness and capacity to choose, we will be imperfect. Kahneman, for example, noted after a life of study and practice that we still need others to see ourselves. This is a role our family and group members help to play, but it can also be facilitated by a coach. You can even think of a coach as a personal trainer for your System 2! Coaching skills and tools are often intended to interrupt our fast processing, such as emotions (more on those later) and System 1 thinking, and shift us into System 2 so that we can slow down and make more intentional choices that align our actions to our goals.

 Experience it yourself

For the next week, try the practice of first noticing when you label something. It could be anything from recognizing the four-legged animal in front of you as a dog to wondering to yourself why your significant other is in such a bad mood. Each time you notice a label, shift to curiosity. How does leaving open the possibility that it's not a dog (maybe you're the first to discover a new species!) or that your partner isn't in a mood but might have just experienced something terrible change what or how you pay attention? Journal about what you notice.

I get so emotional

"He makes me so mad!" Perhaps similar words have come out of your mouth. They have for most of us. But are they true? Can another person control your emotions or "make you" feel something? Emotions are a complex state of feeling that results in physical and psychological changes that influence our thoughts and behaviors.[9] Scientists disagree about the nature and basis of emotions.[10] Some believe they are evolutionary or biologically based.[11] Others argue that they are both socially constructed and culture specific.[12] Despite these areas of disagreement, there is general agreement that emotions are associated with subjective feelings, physiological responses, and expressive behavior. Emotions influence our thoughts and behavior. They can be rich sources of data for us to better understand ourselves. They also have a huge influence on how we interact with others. They impact how our actions and intentions are perceived by others and how others respond to us.

There's evidence that facial expressions corresponding to a set of basic emotions – anger, contempt, disgust, fear, joy, sadness, and surprise – are universal.[13] This suggests that even when other barriers such as language and cultural norms obscure our ability to understand each other, basic emotions and how we display them help us communicate across cultural lines. While this is probably a good thing, our emotions can sometimes betray us. Because emotions are such powerful forces, we've evolved to be highly sensitive to them.[14]

Although people often develop an ability to control or manipulate our verbal displays of emotion, our bodies or non-verbal behaviors often give them away – something referred to as emotional leakage. Emotions give us data about ourselves and about other people, which can serve to identify threats and help us navigate social dynamics (something that was critical to our survival). It may not surprise you that emotions are also contagious (emotion contagion).[15] In fact, it's not just transient emotions but depression, anxiety, and stress spread through a process called social contagion[16] and there's evidence that people in managerial or leadership positions can have a disproportionate impact on those around them. For example, human transformation company, BetterUp, found that leaders who are in the top quartile on their emotional regulation have subordinates who report being 21% higher in emotional regulation themselves and have 14% higher emotional thriving overall.[17]

Emotions exert a powerful influence on our thoughts and behavior. The words "triggered," "hooked," or "hijacked" are often used to describe an experience of powerful emotion clouding our ability to think reasonably and rationally, resulting in thoughts, words, or actions that we may not have intended or later regret. Emotional reactions are fast and powerful. Our brains are hard-wired to react quickly to situations that feel threatening. Fast emotional reactions are a survival mechanism. The problem is, your brain has not evolved to discern the difference between a grizzly bear staring you down and a terse and intimidating email from your boss. To our brains, a threat is a threat.

Your amygdala lights up with activity, and your brain is flooded with powerful emotions that prompt you to fight, flee, or freeze up. Here's a mundane, but hopefully relatable example. You're waiting in a long line to check out at the grocery store. Suddenly, another shopper with a full cart pulls up to the register and starts unloading their groceries to check out. Then you feel it . . . the rush of anger. This is a violation of the rules and your expectations, and a personal affront to you as you were patiently waiting your turn. Perhaps your immediate reaction is to fight: "Hey – what are you doing? There's a line back here!" (said with a piercing glare and some hands of disbelief). Or maybe you get flustered and quickly move along to another checkout line to avoid confrontation. Or maybe you're a "freezer" and just stand and stare at the other person, wondering what just happened. If you live in a place where you don't have to wait in line at the grocery store, you can probably relate to another example: Waiting patiently for a parking space at the mall and someone else snatches it from you. Didn't they see your turn signal? Who do they think they are?

Fortunately, science has also identified useful coping strategies for moving past these powerful emotional reactions. **Pausing** – the magical moment that helps you make better choices – is a great option. You've probably heard the advice to "count to 10" when you are angry. That's a pause practice. Emotions are fast. Cognition is slower. A pause allows time for cool, rational thought to catch up to that hot emotion. In the example above, choosing to pause for a moment might help you avoid a reaction that escalates the situation. One common reaction when someone cuts in line or steals your parking space is to commit **the Fundamental Attribution Error** (FAE),[18] which is when we attribute people's behavior to their personality, rather than the circumstances. The FAE is another one of those mental shortcuts and cognitive biases we fall prey to. The other person is what stands out most to us in a situation, not the surrounding circumstances – particularly those we cannot see. Therefore, we attribute the frustrating situation to something undesirable about the other person – they are a jerk, they are selfish, entitled, etc. FAE reactions occur lightning fast. Think about a time someone cut you off in traffic. It probably didn't take long for you to honk your horn and think or say, "What an asshole!" That was pure emotion, pure reaction – no deliberate thought needed!

Here's where that pause practice becomes so powerful. If we can **notice** that we are experiencing a strong emotional reaction we can choose to **pause** and let cognition catch up, before simply falling prey to our typical stimulus-response reactions. In the instance of the grocery store line-cutter, taking 10 seconds to pause gives us the time and space to make a deliberate choice about how we want to react. Once you have noticed, you can use the **Name and Reframe** technique. Yes, you might have that immediate angry, affronted reaction, but by inserting a pause, you can name that emotion: "I am feeling angry and disrespected." Psychiatrist and mindfulness expert Dan Siegel has found in his research that naming our emotions leaves us more equipped to manage them. As Siegel puts it, we can "name it to tame it."[19] When you pause to notice the emotion you are experiencing, then say out loud what you are experiencing, you create space and distance between yourself and that emotion. You empower yourself by moving from *being* the emotion, where it has you (e.g., "*I am angry*"), to having the emotion (e.g., "*I feel angry*").

Recent research has also shown that *stopping* at naming our emotions has a risk of letting those feelings crystalize.[20] Once we have recognized our emotion, tools like reframing and cognitive reappraisal play an important role in what we do next. Cognitive reappraisal means pausing to recognize our negative thought patterns and choosing something else instead that serves us better. For instance, instead of rushing into the thoughts and actions that might follow from that anger, we can choose to say, "Do I really care? This will only be five minutes." Or we can assume positive intent. We can think graceful and kind thoughts like "maybe they really need to use the bathroom" or "maybe they just got a call that they have to pick up their sick kid from school." Come up with whatever explanation you want. In fact, have fun with it. This act of reframing opens up additional possibilities regarding what did and can happen and creates the opportunity to choose how you want to respond (also note the similarities between this and stereotypes or labels).

Researchers at Harvard University recently demonstrated that using two specific forms of reappraisal, called *reconstrual* and *repurposing*, can lead to significant reductions in negative emotions *and* significant increases in positive emotions.[21] Reconstrual is one form of reappraisal in which someone deliberately changes their mental construal of a situation to drive a more desirable emotional response, much like reframing. The slightly different reappraisal strategy of *repurposing* asks participants to focus on the potentially positive *outcomes* of the situation, thereby also resulting in a more positive emotional response. These researchers studied participants' emotional responses to challenging situations related to COVID-19, which has increased negative emotions for people of all backgrounds around the globe. They found that participants who used either of these two reappraisal strategies experienced more positive emotions and decreased negative emotions in response to their experiences with the pandemic, quarantine, and lockdowns. Both reappraisal strategies had equally positive impact for participants, who were able to think differently about challenging experiences they were facing. For example, let's say you were feeling isolated, trapped, and sad about quarantining during the early days of the pandemic. One way to *reconstrue* this experience would be to say, "You know, I've always wanted to learn how to make sourdough bread and read the entire Harry Potter series. This is my opportunity!" If you were practicing *repurposing*, you would focus on the health and safety impacts of quarantine – such as, "By quarantining and staying home, I am doing what I can to keep my family safe and healthy." The whole point of reframing and reappraisal is to break the stimulus-response cycle that causes ourselves and others pain by getting all worked up about something that might not really matter that much. You may not be able to stop your brain from having that initial flood of emotion, but you can *notice* it, *pause*, and *make a deliberate choice* about how you want to respond. This ability to be aware of our emotions and to control them so that we can express them in healthy ways is referred to as emotional agility.[22]

In her book *Taking the Leap*, Buddhist monk Pema Chödrön asks, "Which wolf do we want to feed?" She notes that within each of us we have a wolf of patience and courage and a wolf of aggression and violence. We all possess this duality, and when we allow emotions, pride, fear, or the need to be right to guide our behavior, we are feeding the wrong wolf. The wolf of kindness, patience, and grace is starved when we choose not to feed them. By becoming aware of our own reactions and tendencies and choosing to pause, we create space and opportunity to choose which wolf we feed.

Emotions are data. How we feel about a situation, particularly when we're having a negative reaction, can help illuminate what's most important to us – our values. Your values are your guiding principles. They are the things that are most important to you across situations.

1. What are your top 3–5 values? There are many lists of values to pull from and approaches to help you explore what matters most to you. We recommend starting by not overthinking it. Just review the list and notice what words resonate most with you. It can be helpful to start with making a list of 10 values and continuing to narrow in on those you just can't bear to cross off the list.

Achievement	Humility	Independence
Power	Caring	Excitement
Safety	Dependability	Adventure
Tradition	Nature	Acceptance
Approval	Tolerance	Accountability
Recognition	Advancement	Agility
Authenticity	Balance	Beauty
Competition	Bravery	Candor
Challenge	Collaboration	Comfort
Commitment	Community	Confidence
Conformity	Creativity	Curiosity
Learning	Discipline	Status

2. Think of a situation that feels challenging or where you are experiencing negative emotions. What is the hardest part of the situation for you? What is the most upsetting? How does that connect with your values?
3. Reframe the situation from what you are against to what you are for. That is, how does the situation illustrate what you are committed to?
4. Create a plan for how you will address the situation in a way that reinforces your commitment to your values.

What this might look like for Tanielle:

Values: Achievement, Recognition, Candor

Situation: The hardest part for Tanielle was that she felt broadsided by her peer's promotion. She didn't know where she stood in the organization, what her superiors were looking for, and how she measured up against those criteria. She lost trust with her boss and started to question whether she would be able to advance.

Commitment: Tanielle is committed to working hard for the company and seeing the fruits of her labor. She wants a manager who will tell her where she stands and provide feedback and recognition so that she can improve and progress in her career.

Address the situation: Tanielle could have scheduled a one-on-one with her manager after the promotion to ask whether she had been considered for the promotion. She could have used that opportunity to express her interest in advancing in her career and describe what that looks like for her. She could request a commitment from her manager to provide ongoing feedback – positive and negative – on her contributions to enable her growth.

The Matrix is real: How we construct reality

Let's return to our grocery store example. It's not necessarily the case that every person waiting in line would respond to someone cutting in front of them in the same way. There are several things under the surface that help shape our interpretation of events. Concepts like the ladder of inference[23] and constructed reality[24] help to explain how the same event can be interpreted differently across individuals, groups, or even countries. Like all species, humans have evolved for survival. This applies to our biology and to our psychology. Our brains take shortcuts, optimizing for survival, because we'd be overwhelmed by complexity otherwise. We develop emotional and behavioral patterns that serve us during childhood that might get in our way as we have more choices available to us as adults. The conditions that we interact with – everything from the personalities and traditions in our homes to the environmental conditions in our country of origin – influence how we see and respond to ourselves and to the world around us. And, as the saying goes, "the fish can't see the water." It takes intention and/or contrast to step back enough to see how all these invisible forces color your perception.

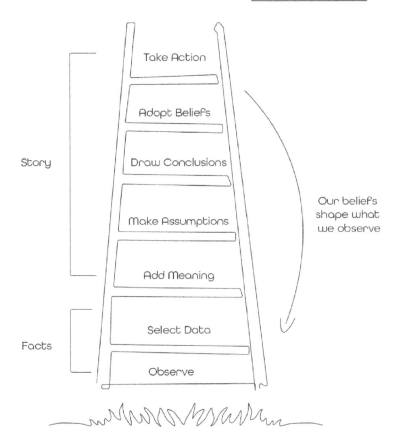

Take Action

Adopt Beliefs

Draw Conclusions

Story

Make Assumptions

Add Meaning

Select Data

Facts

Observe

Our beliefs
shape what
we observe

Source: Adaptation of the ladder of inference, developed by Chris Argyris

In 1970, management scholar Chris Argyris developed the ladder of inference to describe how we move from data to action. This simple tool helps to demonstrate how our values, beliefs, culture, and thoughts form interconnected layers between what is happening around us and our *experience* of what is happening. An important takeaway is that data (or facts) make up a very small part of this process. The rest can be described as "the story" we tell about the data. When we tell stories, we are always the protagonist and the narrator. As we develop greater self-awareness, we become more aware of the story we're telling, how well the story is working for us (or not working for us), and to whom we are assigning power. Coaching can help you edit the story to become more empowered.

The ladder of inference can also be used as a reflection aid to help you or others become more self-aware. For example, you can use it as a structure to stimulate questions up and down the ladder. In fact, let's practice right now.

Experience it yourself

Think of a coworker (or friend, or someone you volunteer with, etc.) that you don't particularly enjoy working with. What judgments or beliefs do you have about them?

_____

_____

_____

Where does that belief come from? What example can you think of that contributed to you forming that belief?

_____

_____

_____

What assumptions were you making about that situation? What else might have been happening?

_____

_____

_____

How will you reframe some of your beliefs and assumptions about your coworker?

_____

_____

_____

What does it mean to wear a mask?

The COVID-19 pandemic provided an unusual opportunity for a global, shared experience. The virus didn't recognize geographic or political boundaries. It spread rapidly and indiscriminately across borders, killing millions of people. Although the virus behaved indiscriminately, people did not. Decisions about how to respond were laden with individual and cultural values, political views, and societal norms. The pandemic brought into focus an underlying tension: should I act in accordance with my own self-interest, favoring individual freedom, or should I act in accordance with the collective good for the most vulnerable among us? One tool to protect against the virus was a mask. While many people readily took to mask wearing, and individuals and companies quickly went into production mode to make them more accessible, others saw masks as a threat to their individual freedoms. Cultural factors, like individualism versus collectivism and tightness versus looseness, influenced these responses. In fact, new research[25] shows that people in more collectivistic areas are more likely to wear masks. The mask is the same anywhere in the world, but the story we tell about the mask and what it means is not.

Now, back to coaching

We can't change what we can't see. A big part of coaching is about helping us see more of what is happening and to shift perspective. In most situations where we feel stuck, we are seeing things in a particular way that leads us to a particular strategy. When that strategy doesn't work, we must be able to step back and reassess so that we can find another path. By understanding how our cognitive biases, emotions, and personal stories can impact our sensemaking, we position ourselves better to employ tools to broaden our perspectives. In other words, a better understanding of how people work, paired with coaching skills, enables us to both see and change what's not working for us.

To explore this further, let's pick up where we left off with the coworker you thought of in the last exercise.

Experience it yourself

Which of your values might be violated in this situation? What are you committed to that you feel is being violated?

_____

_____

_____

How could you be wrong?

_____

_____

_____

How have your feelings toward this person shifted? What are you now curious about?

_____

_____

_____

A coaching mindset

In this chapter, we've focused on better understanding ourselves and how our brains and emotions influence the stories we tell about ourselves, our experiences, and the world around us. Understanding that we do not move through the world objectively is important. None of us has privileged access to the truth. Remembering that basic principle will make it much easier to practice coaching rather than giving advice or problem solving. It helps us to stay open to possibilities, curious about how others are making sense of the world and emboldened by the knowledge that we have more choices than we often realize. Three elements of your "self" are important for your coaching mindset: (1) self-awareness, (2) self-development, and (3) self-regulation.

Self-awareness allows you to see how your own background may have influenced who you are as an individual and how it colors the way you view the world. You understand that what is true or right for you may not work for another person. You become aware of your intuition and the power it can provide to you or to the person you're supporting, but you hold it lightly, knowing it could be wrong or that it might not serve them. **Self-development** builds on self-awareness. It requires having a reflective practice and the desire to engage in ongoing learning so that you are fit to coach. **Self-regulation** refers to being aware of your thoughts and emotions and being able to regulate them to stay calm and present. We'll talk more about mindset in chapters to come.

The International Coaching Federation (ICF)[26] released an updated competency model in January 2021 to define professional coaching. The second competency – *Embodies a Coaching Mindset* – is defined as maintaining a mindset that is open, curious, flexible, and client-centered. It includes the following markers:

- Acknowledges that clients are responsible for their own choices
- Engages in ongoing learning and development as a coach
- Develops an ongoing reflective practice to enhance one's coaching
- Remains aware of and open to the influence of context and culture on self and others
- Uses awareness of self and one's intuition to benefit clients
- Develops and maintains the ability to regulate one's emotions
- Mentally and emotionally prepares for sessions
- Seeks help from outside sources when necessary

This competency was developed to describe how mindset shows up in the role of a professional coach in the context of formal coaching sessions. Yet, any person in any role can adopt a coaching mindset in their day-to-day interactions.

Conclusion

In Chapter 2 we have explored the role of our brains, emotions, and how we process information in the ways that we make sense of our experiences and the world around us. Strengthening your self-awareness and understanding how your brain works are both essential for having more effective interactions with others. We can easily cruise through life on autopilot, not paying much attention to what we are thinking or experiencing or why. Or, we can recognize what is happening with our thoughts and emotions and practice strategies to learn from and better manage those thoughts and emotions. We have a bias toward the latter because it shifts the power from the world outside of our control to the world inside our control.

In the next chapter we will move from thoughts and feelings to behavior. Our thoughts, feelings, and behaviors are inherently interconnected, so this isn't the last you'll read about emotions and cognition. Finally, if you find yourself asking, "what does all of this have to do with using a coaching approach?" remember that a foundation in "self work" is an important first step in using the specific skills and techniques that come later in this book.

Chapter 2 Key idea

Building awareness around your own limitations and realizing that we are all built this way can create the opportunity to be more intentional about the way you experience and show up in the world. This can help you get more of what you want and help others do the same. Beliefs, values, cognitions, and emotions (and ego) feed into how you interpret the world.

Want to learn more? Check out

The *Invisibilia* podcast is produced by National Public Radio (NPR) and includes rich storytelling about the invisible forces that influence our ideas and behavior. You can access the podcast through NPR One, Apple Podcasts, Google Podcasts, Pocket Casts, or Spotify.

Recommended reading

How emotions are made: The secret life of the brain by Lisa Feldman Barrett

Thinking fast and slow by Daniel Kahneman

The whole brain child by Dan Siegel and Tina Payne Bryson

Notes

1 Bohn, R. E., & Short, J. (2009). *How much information? A 2009 report on American consumers*. San Diego: University of California, Global Information Industry Center.

2 Wu, T., Dufford, A. J., Mackie, M. A., Egan, L. J., & Fan, J. (2016). The capacity of cognitive control estimated from a perceptual decision making task. *Scientific Reports, 6*(1), 1–1. https://doi.org/10.1038/srep34025

3 B. R. (2015, January 29). A crash course in probability. *The Economist*. www.economist.com/gulliver/2015/01/29/a-crash-course-in-probability

4 Tversky, A., & Kahneman, D. (1974). Judgment under uncertainty: Heuristics and biases: Biases in judgments reveal some heuristics of thinking under uncertainty. *Science, 185*(4157), 1124–1131. https://doi.org/10.1126/science.185.4157.1124

5 Korteling, J. E., Brouwer, A. M., & Toet, A. (2018). A neural network framework for cognitive bias. *Frontiers in Psychology, 9*(1561), 1–12. https://doi.org/10.3389/fpsyg.2018.01561

6 Kahneman, D. (2011). *Thinking, fast and slow*. New York: Farrar, Straus and Giroux.

7 Merton, R. (1948). The self-fulfilling prophecy. *The Antioch Review, 8*(2), 193–210. https://doi.org/10.2307/4609267

8 Nickerson, R. S. (1998). Confirmation bias: A ubiquitous phenomenon in many guises. *Review of General Psychology, 2*(2), 175–220. https://doi.org/10.1037/1089-2680.2.2.175

9 Barrett, L. F. (2012). Emotions are real. *Emotion, 12*(3), 413–429. https://doi.org/10.1037/a0027555

10 Beck, J. (2015, August 20). Hard feelings: Science's struggle to define emotions. *The Atlantic*. www.theatlantic.com/health/archive/2015/02/hard-feelings-sciences-struggle-to-define-emotions/385711/

11 Ekman, P., & Keltner, D. (1970). Universal facial expressions of emotion. *California Mental Health Research Digest, 8*(4), 151–158.

12 Barrett, L. F. (2006). Solving the emotion paradox: Categorization and the experience of emotion. *Personality and Social Psychology Review, 10*(1), 20–46. https://doi.org/10.1207/s15327957pspr1001_2

13 Matsumoto, D. (2001). Culture and emotion. In D. Matsumoto (Ed.), *The handbook of culture and psychology* (pp. 171–194). New York: Oxford University Press.

14 Martinez, L., Falvello, V. B., Aviezer, H., & Todorov, A. (2016). Contributions of facial expressions and body language to the rapid perception of dynamic emotions. *Cognition and Emotion, 30*(5), 939–952. https://doi.org/10.1080/02699931.2015.1035229

15 Barsade, S., & O'Neill, O. A. (2020, December 16). Manage your emotional culture. *Harvard Business Review*. https://hbr.org/2016/01/manage-your-emotional-culture

16 Kensbock, J. M., Alkærsig, L., & Lomberg, C. (2021). The epidemic of mental disorders in business – How depression, anxiety, and stress spread across organizations through employee mobility. *Administrative Science Quarterly*, 67(1), 1–48. https://doi.org/10.1177/00018392211014819

17 BetterUp. (2021). *BetterUp member data*. San Fransisco, CA: BetterUp.

18 Tetlock, P. E. (1985). Accountability: A social check on the fundamental attribution error. *Social Psychology Quarterly*, 48(3), 227–236. https://doi.org/10.2307/3033683

19 Siegel, D. J., & Payne Bryson, T. (2011). *The whole-brain child: 12 revolutionary strategies to nurture your child's developing mind*. New York, NY: Bantam Books.

20 Nook, E. C., Satpute, A. B., & Ochsner, K. N. (2021). Emotion naming impedes both cognitive reappraisal and mindful acceptance strategies of emotion regulation. *Affective Science*, 2(2), 187–198. https://doi.org/10.1007/s42761-021-00036-y

21 Wang, K., Goldenberg, A., Dorison, C. A., Miller, J. K., Uusberg, A., Lerner, J. S., Gross, J. J., Agesin, B. B., Bernardo, M., Campos, O., & Eudave, L. (2021). A multi-country test of brief reappraisal interventions on emotions during the COVID-19 pandemic. *Nature Human Behavior*, 5(8), 1089–1110. https://doi.org/10.1038/s41562-021-01173-x

22 David, S. (2016). *Emotional agility: Get unstuck, embrace change, and thrive in work and life*. New York, NY: Penguin Random House.

23 Argyris, C. (1976). *Increasing leadership effectiveness*. New York, NY: Wiley Publishing.

24 Berger, P. L., & Luckmann, T. (1966). *The social construction of reality*. New York, NY: Random House.

25 Lu, J. G., Jin, P., & English, A. S. (2021). Collectivism predicts mask use during COVID-19. *Proceedings of the National Academy of Sciences*, 118(23), 1–8. https://doi.org/10.1073/pnas.2021793118

26 International Coaching Federation (2021). *ICF core competencies*. https://coachfederation.org/core-competencies

3
Your motivations and actions

Questions we'll answer in this chapter:

1. What is the relationship between thoughts, feelings, and behavior?
2. What role do goals play in our behavior?
3. How does this relate to coaching?

In Chapter 2 we described the power of our cognitions and emotions. When focused, our mindsets, thoughts, and emotions can propel us toward our goals. Without active attention and regulation, they can lead us to behave in ways that derail our work, our relationships, and more. Our behavior is tightly linked with our thoughts and emotions. Our thoughts and feelings influence our future behavior, and we also develop thoughts, feelings, and interpretations about our behaviors. In Chapter 2 we also introduced the power of a pause as a tool to create more space for choice. This pause is an essential break in the stimulus-response loop that often gets us into trouble when powerful emotions lead us to behave in ways we later regret. In this chapter, we'll take a deeper look at the power of that pause for creating space to choose our behavior and responses in challenging situations. We'll also explore the role of goals (whether explicitly or implicitly set) in driving our behavior.

The power of the pause, part 2

Meet Marcus. Marcus is quick and witty, and he cares deeply about his friends and family. He's also competitive and thrives on being a top producer at work. Ask any one of his friends, family, or colleagues about Marcus and they'll gush about him. With one exception: Marcus tends to react strongly. For decades in his work and life, Marcus has had a major blow-up at least

DOI: 10.4324/9781003166917-4

once per week. Something will trigger him, and he "loses it" or "flies off the handle," according to those close to him. Recent triggers for Marcus have included a colleague sending the wrong document to a client, his child spilling a glass of orange juice all over the breakfast table, and a conversation with an old friend about conflicting political views. It's clear when he's triggered: his face turns red, his eyes widen, his fists clench, and he verbally tears into whomever is on the other side of the trigger. Lucky for Marcus, he recovers quickly. Within moments of his outbursts, he's back to normal. His parasympathetic nervous system[1] kicks in, and he's back to his work, his breakfast, or his quality time with friends. Unfortunately, those who are on the receiving end of his reactions don't always have the same experience. Friends, family, and colleagues often feel attacked or shell-shocked, particularly the first time they experience one of Marcus's episodes. While those who have known him for a long time have grown to anticipate and deal with his reactions, others are less accepting.

Recently, Marcus started working with a new leader in his organization. This leader has zero tolerance for aggressive behavior, particularly from a seasoned professional like Marcus, who should be role-modeling and developing others. Marcus receives some "change . . . or else" feedback from this leader. He starts working with a coach, who helps Marcus better understand his reaction patterns and supports him in deciding what he wants to do about them. Marcus begins with simple noticing. He considers this "data collection" to better understand when, where, and why he gets triggered and has these reactive outbursts. As he gains self-awareness around this behavior, he discovers that the trigger is usually a last straw or tipping point in a series of stressful events. For example, when he blew up at his son for spilling juice at the breakfast table, he was already primed. He had been ruminating on a frustrating work call the evening before, which led to poor sleep that night. In the morning he received an email rescheduling an important meeting he'd been preparing for extensively. The spilled juice pushed him over the edge, and all the angst and frustration that had been mounting since the night before came roaring out of his mouth, aimed at his son. When Marcus realized this, he felt a wave of shame and regret – two very powerful emotions that can be hard to endure.

Marcus is motivated to break the pattern of reacting when he's triggered. He experiments with a few techniques to insert a "pause" between the stimulus and response. Marcus first recalls the advice he learned as a kid: to count to 10 when he's angry. This works okay for him, but he finds that reminding himself to count to 10 sometimes annoys him even more. Next, he tries a tactic that he read about in an online article, to take three deep breaths before reacting. While he enjoys the act of intentionally taking three deep breaths, he feels a little uncomfortable doing this in work situations. Taking three deep breaths in a meeting feels weird to him, and he thinks it takes too long. As a result, he feels self-conscious when he uses this tactic. Finally, Marcus takes a piece of advice from his tennis coach to try out a mantra. One day in a staff meeting – after another bad night of sleep and a frustrating commute – he feels his blood pressure rising and notices a reaction coming on in response to a half-baked presentation from one of his team members. Just before he blows up at the team member, he remembers the mantra he came up with: "Stop. Wait. Don't react." This one works for him. It's a pithy and easy reminder that feels meaningful to him and helps him raise his awareness of what he's feeling and the possible action that could follow. He's surprised how well it works. The mantra was easy enough to remember in the heat of the moment and created just enough space for him to pause, notice, cool off, and choose a more constructive response.

In the example above, Marcus discovered how to **use his powers of self-awareness and self-management to slow down, pause, notice his emotions, and make a conscious choice about how to respond.**

Many of us have deeply entrenched patterns of reactions and behaviors that may not be serving us. But the way you respond in a situation does not have to be deterministic. When you notice and become more aware of your own patterns, you create space and opportunity to choose a new way of responding. This ability to choose sits within the prefrontal cortex of your brain. As neuro-endocrinologist Robert Sapolsky explains in his book *Behave*,[2] the prefrontal cortex (PFC) is responsible for decision making, working memory, emotion regulation, and impulse control, among other things. In other words, your PFC is the hub of your ability to choose your behaviors and self-manage. This contrasts with your "monkey brain" – a Buddhist concept that refers to a mind that is unsettled, restless, easily distracted, but can be quieted and controlled through self-regulation and, of course, meditation.

The development of your PFC is not complete until your mid-twenties, which means that there are times in your early life when you genuinely lack the capacity to make certain smart choices or think long term. Once you reach adulthood and the PFC is fully developed, you possess the ability to try on or test out new behaviors to see what will lead to your desired impact on others and the situation. To do that, you must first recognize that you can choose; you don't have to simply act from your "monkey brain," ruled by impulses and stimulus-response triggers.

Take a few minutes now to reflect on some of your own patterns.

Experience it yourself

Think of a situation where you felt "triggered" and reacted in a way you might have later regretted. (Reflect)

_____

_____

_____

What was it about that situation that provoked you? (Notice)

_____

_____

_____

How did you know you were triggered? (Self-awareness)

_____

_____

_____

How would you rather show up in or handle situations like that one? (Choose your behavior)

_____

_____

_____

What will you try next time to create a pause that gives you time and space to choose that more effective response? (Pause practice)

_____

_____

_____

This process of becoming aware of our reactions, noticing what triggers those reactions, inserting a pause practice, and choosing a different behavior or response can be used in a wide variety of situations. How does your ability to keep your cool vary across situations? If you find yourself reacting to and mistreating people who work in service roles (restaurant servers, store clerks, call center operators, etc.), what's prompting your response? Perhaps you are triggered from a tough day at work or frustration with a family member, but you let some automatic reactions slip because you don't think these exchanges are important enough to demand your full attention and self-control. Perhaps you have one coworker who just drives you crazy and provokes reactions that you later regret. In coaching conversations, professional coaches often walk their clients through a process of becoming more self-aware through reflection and feedback. As we discussed in Chapter 2, "noticing" is a simple yet powerful way to collect data on yourself, your tendencies and patterns, and your behavior; coaches often assign "noticing" as homework in between coaching sessions.

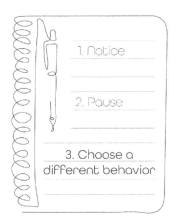

Deliberately choosing new behaviors to try out or experiment with is a common practice in coaching. The key is that a client must be committed and willing to test out those behaviors and notice the impact. This is akin to the process of experiential learning, where we try something out, get some feedback on the impact (either direct feedback or by gauging others' responses or behavior), and reflect on what just happened. It's also common for someone working with a coach to explore pause practices that help them create space to practice self-awareness, noticing, reflection, and choosing their behavior or response.

This process of intentionally choosing our behavior is known as *behavior regulation*. Behavior regulation, or self-regulation, is an ever-present process of making choices that move us toward things that we want (or who we want to be) and away from outcomes that we do not want (or who we do not want to be).[3]

These choices can have both short-term and long-term implications. For example, Marcus chooses to pause and respond in calmer and more constructive ways than he has in the past. The short-term impact of this behavior may be a more peaceful and effective conversation, but the long-term impact of his self-regulated behavior over time could be stronger relationships and increased trust with his family and colleagues. Another short-term impact that Marcus experiences may be fatigue. Regulating our behavior and exercising self-control takes energy and effort. For Marcus, that effort is worthwhile because he has a deep desire to improve his relationships and his impact on others. Whether we realize it or not, goals play an essential part in our self-regulation. Those outcomes that we want to gain or avoid are goals that guide our choices and behavior. These goals may be explicitly stated ("I want to have better relationships with my colleagues and family") or implicit (a desire to avoid discomfort in a conversation, even if we don't explicitly set that goal).

Journaling as a Tool for Self-awareness

As we've described, there's great power in noticing and observing patterns. One easy and inexpensive tool to facilitate that process is a journal. Whether it's an old-fashioned bound journal or a notes application on your smartphone, journaling is a great way to improve your self-awareness and well-being. It's a tool we use in our own development, with our students, and with our coaching clients. The practice can even be applied to work through learning memos and after-action reviews. Here are a few of the benefits of journaling:[4,5]

- Helps clarify thoughts and feelings
- Increases self-awareness
- Reduces stress by processing emotions and improves memory
- Leads to more effective problem solving by accessing analytical and creative parts of your brain
- Helps you track patterns, trends, improvements, and growth over time
- Facilitates learning by stimulating recall and reflection on experience through active retrieval and elaboration

There are many different types of journaling. You can try something structured that includes prompts or something unstructured like a blank page. You can write in bullets or paragraphs, and write for minutes or hours. You can even abandon writing altogether in favor of drawing pictures that capture how you're feeling or what is on your mind. The important thing is to approach the task with curiosity rather than judgment. Creating a practice of reflecting on prior journal entries can help you notice patterns and develop deeper self-awareness.

The role of goals

We have an infinite number of possibilities for how we will behave in any given situation. Almost everything we do is governed not just by our conscious thoughts and processes but a litany of unconscious processing.[6] All behavior is driven by goals, whether consciously stated or not. Let's explore a few different scenarios to help illustrate this bold statement.

- You notice a grumbling in your stomach and make yourself a sandwich.
- You schedule a coffee chat with a colleague from another part of the company.
- You give your child a hug before bed.

Each of these examples reflects a mundane behavior. It might be something you've done a thousand times before, somewhat automatically. And yet, we would argue that each behavior was done in pursuit of one or more goals. The goal could be anything from biological (e.g., ingesting calories to stay alive) to aspirational (e.g., networking to facilitate achievement, recognition, or affiliation). Personal goals are thoughts about the future, and they tend to be emotionally charged. They are meaningful to us and are shaped by our culture, values, and past experiences.[7] Becoming consciously aware of your goals makes it easier to align your behavior with those goals. It's the emotional connection we have to our goals that makes them so powerful in directing our behavior. For instance, you feel excited and energized as you come closer to achieving an important personal growth goal. Or you feel a strong sense of frustration when something is getting in the way of achieving a goal. Our emotions are an excellent source of data. Noticing your frustration may help you identify the thing that is impeding your goal progress, which then helps you come up with creative workarounds to get past the impediment. Tuning into our emotions can help us to bring our subconscious goals into view.

Once more, you might be asking yourself what all of this has to do with coaching. At a foundational level, the purpose of coaching is to help close the gap between where you are and where you want to be. "Where you want to be" is another way of describing your goal. Much of coaching then is about helping to clarify three things – what you want, where you are, and what steps you can take to move from the current to the desired reality.

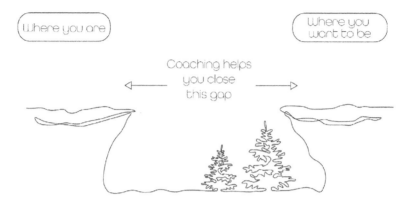

To bring this into focus, let's go back to Marcus. Marcus had an extreme reaction to what was a relatively minor event – his colleague sent the wrong document to a client. Marcus got very angry. His anger led him to snap at and belittle his colleague. In the moment, he felt justified. It was an important client, and that kind of mistake can degrade trust and confidence, ultimately risking revenue for the company.

What goals might have been motivating Marcus? Marcus values achievement and wants to be the best. It could be that Marcus fears that a mistake like this one reflects poorly on him and may threaten his superiority. Alternatively, it could be that Marcus values being the financial provider for his family and fears that loss of revenue could cost him his job or his income, threatening his security and ability to provide. This is where coaching skills and mindset can come in.

Identifying events that cause a strong emotional charge is the first step in digging deeper and uncovering *what the REAL issue is*, such as the goal that is driving your behavior. Gaining clarity on the real issue and the underlying goal enables us to identify other behaviors that might help you achieve that goal, and the connection to other goals that you hold. In Marcus's case, if his underlying goal is to be seen as the top performer, belittling his colleague might make that colleague less likely to make another mistake, but it will likely also hurt Marcus's reputation and reduce the likelihood that others will want to work with him, which could impact his progress on other goals. Realizing this, Marcus can choose another path, such as addressing the mistake directly with the client, providing corrective feedback to his colleague, or using this experience to develop a new approach to checking each other's work to minimize mistakes in the future.

Goals play an important role in directing our energy and are therefore an important focus of coaching. Anytime you are working toward a goal, there is a gap between where you are and where you want to be. Everything in between – behavior, feedback, progress, interference – provokes emotions. Thoughts and emotions are supported by interdependent neural processes, meaning that emotions help us build memories, analyze complex ideas, and make meaningful decisions.[8]

Goals serve three core purposes in directing our behavior: evaluation, commitment, and maintenance. First, we evaluate whether to act and pursue a goal largely based on feelings and emotions tied to that goal. This can happen consciously, particularly when dealing with complex or important goals, or so quickly that we don't even realize it's happening. We decide whether to pursue a goal based on factors such as its relevance to the context, our belief that we can be successful (referred to as efficacy or confidence), and the strength and direction of our emotions related to the goal. In the commitment phase, when a goal has been positively evaluated, it becomes an intention and helps to direct our energy toward planning and problem solving. Finally, goals help to maintain our energy in the face of internal and external obstacles, distractions, and setbacks. That is, as we pursue a goal, we begin to get feedback in the form of the presence or absence of progress. While the initial decision to behave in alignment with our goal is based on our expectation of the result (i.e., we think it will get us somewhere we want to be or help us stay away from somewhere we don't want to be), continuing to engage in that behavior shifts our internal calculus from expectations to experience.[9] Our ability to stay committed to a goal in the face of obstacles is a function of how important it is to us to begin with, our belief that we can accomplish it despite setbacks, and the amount of energy and resources we have to apply to it. This explains why we are more vulnerable to old habits when we are not at our best – for example, when we are hungry, angry, lonely, tired (HALT) or otherwise depleted.

Our ability to self-regulate throughout this process is what helps us to stay motivated throughout the maintenance phase of goal pursuit. Self-regulation involves altering our inner states or responses – overriding one response in favor of a more desirable one.[10] Self-regulation is aided by self-awareness (you can't change what you can't see) and goal clarity (you won't change without a compelling reason). For example, say you have a goal of running a marathon for your fortieth birthday. This goal is multifaceted: on one level you have the goal of completing a marathon. On another level you have a goal of being in

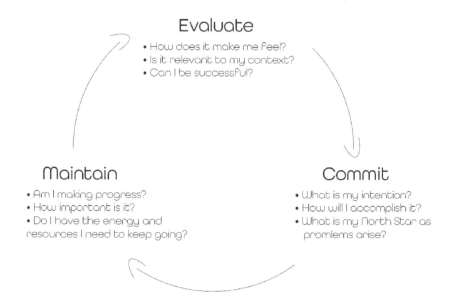

Evaluate

- How does it make me feel?
- Is it relevant to my context?
- Can I be successful?

Maintain

- Am I making progress?
- How important is it?
- Do I have the energy and resources I need to keep going?

Commit

- What is my intention?
- How will I accomplish it?
- What is my North Star as problems arise?

excellent physical condition for a major milestone birthday. It's not unusual for someone training for a marathon to do long runs very early in the morning. Let's say one summer Saturday you set your alarm for 5:30 am to get up for a 14-mile run. You're motivated Friday night when you set that alarm, but Saturday at 5:30 is a little different. The alarm goes off and you are very tempted to stay in bed. Here's where the magic of self-regulation kicks in. You are aware of your desire to turn off the alarm and stay in bed, but that desire is overridden by your desire to achieve your goal of completing a marathon for your birthday. Self-regulation allows us to monitor our behavior and choose a behavior that is in service of our goals, both large and small.

Anti-goals

If you're like us, you love a good to-do list. You get that hit of dopamine every time you cross something off. Those little victories feel so good.

Recently we came across a new kind of list: a "to don't" list. Your to-don't list is exactly what it sounds like: you make a list of all of the things that you don't want to do.

We've found this helpful during our mutual struggle to set boundaries, stop people pleasing, and learn to say "no" (and also remember that

"No." is a complete sentence). For example, a few items on our individual to-don't lists include:

1. Don't schedule back-to-back meetings
2. Don't say "yes" to something until you have thought about it for 24 hours
3. Don't have your email open all day long
4. Don't feel responsible for other people's needs or requests

And so on.

In a way, our to-don't list consists of our anti-goals. If we have a goal of being calm and present during the workday, we might support this with a micro-goal of having 15 minutes between Zoom calls to jot down notes, send a quick follow-up email, grab a snack, or – heaven forbid – use the restroom. Defining what we DON'T do can help us have more clarity and the ability to recognize when we are about to do something counter to our goals.

The tricky thing about to-don't lists and anti-goals is that they can backfire. Research has shown that when we think about what we don't want, we unintentionally activate in our minds the very thing we don't want to think about. For example, if we say, "Don't think about pink elephants," what is the first thing you think about? Probably pink elephants.

When creating a to-don't list or anti-goals, be sure you have commensurate positively framed to-dos and goals you *want* to achieve. We share an example of what this can look like ("This, not that") in Chapter 7. Spend most of your time thinking about what you want to accomplish. Visualize success. Identify specific steps you need to take to make those goals a reality. And use your anti-goals to help you get clear about what you don't want and identify potential challenges you might encounter in your goal pursuit.

Coaching for clarity and commitment

As we mentioned earlier, sometimes we set goals intentionally and explicitly, and we also have implicit goals that we might not pay much attention to or think of as goals. For instance, you might have an explicit goal of brushing your teeth every night before you go to bed, but the underlying implicit goal – which you may not think about every night when you go to brush – is to have good dental hygiene and to prevent future painful dental procedures. That is a goal you hold, that drives your behavior, but not one that you think about explicitly every night before bed. Goals become less straightforward when they are not clear and when we hold competing goals. Goal clarity is important for driving behaviors in support of the goal. When we have total clarity on what we want to achieve and why, we're much more likely to be motivated to work toward that goal and identify specific steps to help us advance closer to our goals.

It's not unusual for coaches to push their clients to get clear on their goals and why they matter. In fact, one of the International Coach Federation's[11] core competencies for coaches is to "acknowledge and support client autonomy in the design of goals, actions, and methods of accountability." Coaches also work with their clients to identify specific next steps or actions to advance progress toward those goals. Big goals, even when they are crystal clear, can feel daunting, or we may not know where to start. Identifying specific first or next steps – such as establishing micro-goals along the way or making "implementation intentions,"[12] which are micro-behaviors – can help move the needle on goal progress in a way that feels manageable and achievable.

Going back to our marathon training example, that 14-mile Saturday run is an example of a micro-goal. Simply saying "I'm going to run 26.2 miles" without a plan is unlikely to lead to successful completion of a marathon. Setting micro-goals along the way that break training down into manageable milestones is much more likely to result in the appropriate training, preparation, and completion of the marathon. When waking up at 5:30 am to run that 14-mile training run feels daunting, implementation intentions can help. Implementation intentions are very specific micro behaviors, often framed as "if, then" statements, or "when this, then that." For example, implementation intentions for getting up at 5:30 am to run 14 miles might include:

- When my alarm goes off at 5:30am, I will get up without hitting snooze.
- When I get up, I will chug a bottle of water.
- After I chug a bottle of water, I will put on my running clothes.
- Once I put on my running clothes, I will do my stretches.
- After I do my stretches, I will eat a snack and grab my gear for the run.
- When the clock strikes 6 am, I will head out the door.

These specific, simple implementation intentions pave the way for starting on some of our most daunting goals. Understanding yourself, including your needs, values, and preferences, can help you to design ways to further motivate yourself along the way. For example, you might have realized that running with friends helps pass the time during a long run and that you look forward to the opportunity for social connection. Planning to meet friends for that long run can help you resist the urge to hit snooze by layering additional goals on top of your micro-goals to amplify your motivation.

Coaching for maintenance and accountability

Many coaches encourage their clients to create development plans that help the client get clear about the goals they want to achieve, as well as anticipate some of the challenges they might encounter and how they will start moving in the right direction. One of the most essential inputs for monitoring progress toward our goals is feedback. Though many people bristle at the mere mention of the word, feedback is essential for gauging progress between our current state and our desired state (goal). Without feedback – which can come from other people, ourselves, or the environment – we operate in a vacuum, without awareness or markers of how effectively we are closing the gap between where we are today and where we want to be.[13] Feedback and coaching are intimately intertwined. Coaches may share direct feedback and observations with the client. They can also be a thought partner to a client thinking through feedback they have received, all in the service of moving closer to their goals.

For example, meet Veronica, who had a goal of feeling more confident speaking up in leadership team meetings. Her current state was that she waited too long and overthought what she wanted to say, to the extent that she missed her window to speak up. By the time she was ready to chime in, the group had already moved on to another topic. Veronica's coach worked with her to gain deeper self-awareness around what was happening in those moments, and what she WANTED to happen in those moments. Veronica practiced noticing her own behavior during leadership team meetings to develop even more self-awareness and realized that her self-doubt and inner monologue were getting in her way of contributing. She set a micro-goal of speaking up when she had an idea before she had a chance to overthink it. She experimented with this in a leadership team meeting, and then paid attention to what happened. She felt nervous and excited about her contribution, and got reinforcing feedback from her colleagues. They praised her idea in the moment and built on it further. Later, her manager made a point to acknowledge the value of Veronica's comment. In this example, Veronica has a clear goal, and she's aware of where she stands and what's in her way. She sets micro-goals, takes a step out of her comfort zone, and receives feedback that indicates she's moving in the right direction.

Experience it yourself

Pause for a moment to think about some of the goals that you have right now. Some are probably explicit ("I want to finish reading this book," "I have a goal of saving $100,000 for a down payment on a house"), and some are implicit (setting your alarm for 6 am and then actually getting up when the alarm goes off, not getting heart disease). Try to think of 10 goals that you currently have, in any part of your work and life:

1. _____

2. _____

3. _____

4. _____

5. _____

6. _____

7. _____

8. _____

9. _____

10. _____

What do you notice about your goals? Which have you set explicitly? Which are implicit or assumed?

_____

_____

_____

What impact have these goals had on your behavior and your choices recently?

_____

_____

_____

Which goals are you most motivated to pursue? Why?

_____

_____

_____

Which goals are you least motivated to pursue? Why?

_____

_____

_____

What are your "anti-goals"?

_____

_____

_____

Choose one goal from your list. Practice breaking it down into smaller micro-goals or implementation intentions.

_____

_____

_____

Earlier we mentioned another common challenge: competing goals. Competing goals can cause us a great sense of conflict, indecisiveness, and confusion. The challenge with competing goals is that they pull our behavior in different directions. For example, say you have two goals: establishing better work/life balance and getting promoted. Your goal of better work/life balance might lead you to make choices like logging off at 6 pm, not working on the weekends, and taking a lunch break. But your goal of getting promoted demands behaviors like taking on additional stretch work assignments, being highly responsive to your boss who works around the clock and over the weekends, and traveling 25% more. Holding these two goals simultaneously may lead to you feeling frustrated and conflicted because they are pulling your behavior in two different directions.

Outside of work, you may hold competing goals of (1) spending time with friends and (2) saving money. To pursue your goal of spending more time with friends, you participate in happy hours, dinners out, and weekend getaway trips. You enjoy seeing your friends, but also feel angst every time you spend money on these activities because you are working against your goal of saving. Next time you notice yourself feeling frustration or angst as you make choices or take actions in support of one goal, pause to ask yourself if you have another goal – explicit or implicit – that is at odds with the first goal and demands a different set of behaviors and choices.[14] If you discover that you do hold competing goals, you have some choices to make, including integrating, revising, or even abandoning one or both of those goals.

Leaving space to change directions

It's easy to get locked into goals that we set, continuing to push ourselves in pursuit of them even if we aren't making the progress we'd like. When you set your own goals, you have discretion to revisit or revise those goals as conditions evolve. For example, in early 2020 you set a goal to visit a new country every year. And then, three months into the year, COVID-19 rendered that goal unachievable for 2020. You could fiercely clutch on to that goal, despite the changing world conditions (which were completely out of your control), or you could choose to adapt that goal to match the changing circumstances. Instead of trying to visit a new country in 2020, you could have revised that goal to try food from five different countries that you'd never had before. And perhaps in revising that goal, you established a new one: supporting local restaurants in your community that were dealt a very difficult blow from the COVID lockdowns.

In addition to revising our goals, sometimes simply abandoning our goals can be adaptive. For many people this feels like heresy – once they commit to a goal, they pursue it relentlessly, no matter what. But the reality is, our context is always changing: your work conditions, life, information available to you, your other goals and desires. Holding firm to a goal that no longer serves you will likely leave you feeling unmotivated and frustrated.

Let's go back to our birthday marathon example. Say you set this goal but have never enjoyed running. You start with your marathon training program, gradually building up to longer and longer training runs. And you hate it. You absolutely dread that 14-mile training run on Saturday morning. The night before, you are filled with dread. You are cranky and snap at your partner even though they have nothing to do with your goal. You turn down invitations to fun parties and events because you must wake up early for your run. During your run you are miserable and ask yourself why the heck you decided to run a marathon. You have a choice: you can continue to pursue this goal and hate every moment of it until the marathon is complete, or you can say, "You know, I thought I would enjoy this. I've put a lot of effort into training, but I have no desire to continue. What I really wanted was to feel great in my body at this milestone. I think for my fortieth birthday I'd rather set a new goal of saving money for a spa weekend where I can get a massage and a facial, and just relax." You can frame this example either as abandoning your goal of running a marathon, because it no longer serves you, or as revising your goal to something that you care more about as a celebration of your birthday. There might be multiple paths to what you really want. You can choose a path that also feels good to you.

Research Spotlight:

James W. Beck, PhD, Associate Professor of Psychology at the University of Waterloo, on competing goals

Us: James, why are you interested in studying competing goals?

Dr. Beck: The idea that goals are in competition is important for understanding why people behave in the ways they do. For instance, I study workplace safety. A common question that arises regarding unsafe work behaviors is: *If unsafe behaviors can result in accidents and injuries, then why do people behave unsafely in the first place?* Often, the answer to this question is that working the "safe way" is less efficient than taking shortcuts, and safety equipment is uncomfortable.

Us: So, people have other goals, like getting work done quickly and being comfortable, that compete with their safety goals, like avoiding accidents.

Dr. Beck: Yes, and you have to weigh these competing goals to understand the choices people make regarding how to allocate their time and effort at work.

Us: What's another example?

Dr. Beck: I recently published a study with colleagues where we looked at managers' competing goals of delivering feedback to a subordinate, plus creating a budget and a schedule by a certain deadline. Whether or not the managers prioritized the feedback conversation depended on how much they thought the subordinate would care about and use the feedback.

Us: The managers went with the goal that they thought would have the most impact?

Dr. Beck: Correct. If the managers thought the feedback would pay off in terms of improved subordinate performance, they prioritized giving feedback. If that seemed like less of a sure bet, they focused their effort on other tasks like creating budgets and schedules. People tend to put their efforts into pursuing goals that most are "in need" or falling behind, but we also weigh the probability of success. If accomplishing one goal is a sure thing, we might not attend to it right away, instead putting our attention where it's most needed. Likewise, we don't put much effort into pursuing a goal with a low likelihood of success because it feels like a lost cause.

Us: James, what role do emotions play in choosing between goals?

Dr. Beck: Our rate of progress towards our goals has a large impact on our emotions. Fast progress feels good, and we feel optimistic that the goal will be achieved. But slow progress can bring on negative emotions like frustration. I have found in my research that when people face slow-downs in their goal progress, they get frustrated and start looking for shortcuts to speed things up, which can create a very unsafe situation. When progress is suddenly slowed, it's important to take a breath and readjust our expectations. Otherwise we risk making bad decisions, like taking shortcuts, in the name of faster progress.

Us: Final question. What can our readers do to better manage multiple goals or competing goals?

Dr. Beck: Become aware of the "planning fallacy," which is when people underestimate how long it takes to achieve a goal or complete a task. Common examples are things like getting your holiday shopping done and completing your taxes. These types of goals consist of several subtasks that need to be accomplished, and there's lots of space for interruptions. For instance, when trying to estimate how long it will take you to do your holiday shopping, do you account for time spent searching for a parking spot at the mall? Do you add a buffer in case your partner texts you asking you to pick up dinner? The point is, when we don't take things like sub-goals or interruptions into account, we tend to underestimate how long things will take. This can make us feel overwhelmed or frustrated, miss deadlines, or let stuff fall through the cracks. But when people are forced to stop and think through these tasks, taking into account all the little sub-tasks and hiccups along the way, they tend to be a lot more accurate in their timing estimates. Pausing to think through and plan for competing demands can help us be much more successful at managing those competing goals when they arise.

Checking in frequently with your goals to ensure they are still relevant and supported by the ever-changing conditions around your work and life will help you maintain clarity around and stay motivated to achieve your goals. Hanging onto a goal that is no longer relevant, realistic, or motivating can lead to negative emotions, like frustration, anger, lack of motivation, and even depression. In their research, Jones and colleagues[15] found that failure to achieve goals led to depressive symptoms and anxiety, and that ruminating on those failures further contributed to the negative emotional experience. Making progress toward something meaningful, known as the progress principle, has a strong positive impact on people's subjective experiences.[16]

Should you find yourself in a similar position – failing to meet a goal, experiencing negative emotions as a result, and ruminating on or judging yourself for that failure – you can use some of the techniques described earlier to help lift you out of that cycle of rumination. Start by noticing how you are feeling in response to your lack of goal attainment. Notice not only your emotions, but also any negative self-talk. Take this opportunity to pause and become more self-aware of your experience. What's getting in the way of making progress on your goals? Are your goals still relevant, realistic, and important to you? Are your goals excessively challenging and therefore unattainable (such as Brodie's childhood dream of playing in the NHL despite not being able to ice skate – and not being a man). Once you have more clarity on what's going wrong with your goal pursuit, you can make a deliberate choice about what to do next, such as changing your behavior to help you make more progress on your goal, revising your goal to be more realistic, identifying and addressing any competing goals, or choosing to abandon your goal if it's no longer serving you. Your negative emotions act as a warning system that something is not working with your goals. And, when there is a gap between where we currently are and where we want to be, we can choose to ramp up efforts to change our current state, move our desired state (goal) closer to our current state (revision), or eliminate that tension by letting go of the goal altogether. Try it for yourself now.

> Your negative emotions act as a warning system that something is not working with your goals.

Experience it yourself

List one goal that is causing you frustration, anxiety, or where you are experiencing lack of progress.

_____

_____

_____

What emotions arise for you when you think about this goal?

_____

_____

_____

To what extent is this goal still relevant, realistic, and important to you?

_____

_____

_____

What changes do you need to make to this goal or a competing goal to help you make progress?

_____

_____

_____

What will you do next? This could include changing your behavior, modifying the goal or competing goals, abandoning the goal, setting achievable milestones, etc.

_____

_____

_____

What emotions do you WANT to feel as you work toward this goal?

_____

_____

_____

Deep grooves

Coaching can be a powerful tool to support behavior change. A coaching client may want to leave behind old habits that are no longer working for them, develop new habits aligned with their goals, or fine-tune a behavior that's important for their work or life. Also, behavior change is hard. Behavior change is hard for the same reason that disrupting our stimulus-response cycle is hard. We get caught up in habits or patterns, and changing those requires BOTH letting go of the old behavior and adopting new behaviors. It takes effort, and one thing we know from Chapter 2 is that our brains prefer the easier route. Social support can facilitate our success.

The behaviors we want to change have typically been reinforced over the years. We sometimes refer to this as habits of patterns of thoughts and behaviors creating "deep grooves." Imagine that you're walking down the beach. Each time you walk down the path, the weight of your feet pushes a bit of the sand to either side, creating a footprint. Over time, if you continue to walk the same path, the groove will get deeper and more embedded. And, the more you walk the same path, the more effortless if becomes. You don't have to make conscious decisions about where to go. It becomes automatic. Taking a different path will require conscious attention and more effort as our body won't be as familiar with all the little bumps along the way.

Some of our gnarliest habits as humans are consistently reinforced, which is why they are hard to abandon. A smoking habit is reinforced not only chemically, through the neurological effect of nicotine, but also socially, by giving smokers a chance to step outside and take a break, to talk and connect with others who are also taking a smoke break. Excessive drinking is hard to curb because we lose our inhibitions in the moment, and because rewarding social activities (happy hours, dance parties, nice dinners) and cues that we are relaxing (a scotch or a beer at the end of a long day) make us feel good and mark important rituals in our lives. Workaholism wreaks havoc on our mental and physical health and relationships, but it is consistently reinforced through praise, rewards, promotions, and achievements at work. To change complex habits like these, we need clear and compelling reasons to choose something else. This change also often requires *unlearning*. As we start to forge a new path, we must train ourselves that the old one isn't taking us to where we want to go. We must believe that it is worth the extra effort and attentional resources to do something different.

Goals play an essential role in behavior change. Having a clear "what" and "why" provides direction and motivation for behavior change. Clearer, more specific goals are more likely to drive behavior, and when those goals are relevant and meaningful to us, we are more motivated to pursue them. Behavior change also requires feedback and time to pause and notice what just happened.

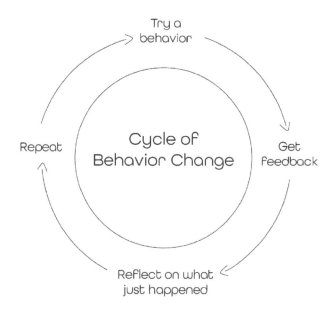

Let's consider workaholism. Meet Andres, who struggles with workaholism and really wants to make meaningful and lasting changes in his life, in support of his physical and mental health, his relationships with friends and family, and because he's getting bored with his unidimensional focus. It's not enough to just say "I don't want to be a workaholic anymore." Andres needs compelling goals to pull his behavior in a new, desired direction, such as a goal of having a more balanced lifestyle (and even better if he can get specific – such as not working before 8 am or after 8 pm; spending one evening per week with friends; getting to the gym four days per week). Andres's current state is – in his words – "workaholism," which includes looking at email the moment he wakes up at 5 am, working on average 14 hours per day and every weekend, and prioritizing work above all else. His desired state is one of greater balance.

To close that gap and start moving toward his desired state, Andres needs to experiment with new behaviors. He must pause to reflect and notice the impact of those new behaviors and get feedback on the effect of his new behaviors. Andres begins by stopping work every Wednesday at 6 pm. He's incredibly anxious and uncomfortable logging off at that time, but he's excited that he is taking a step in the right direction. On his first work-free Wednesday night, Andres deliberately pauses to notice how he feels. He relaxes with his partner by having take-out dinner at home and reading a magazine on the couch while listening to music. In the moment, he notices, "Wow, this feels awesome. Is this what other people's lives are like?"

Andres gets a full eight hours of sleep, and when he wakes up, he notices how refreshed he feels. He's in a good mood, has mental clarity, and is excited and ready to take on the workday. Noticing this feeling he wonders, "Do I feel this way because I didn't work late last night?" Later that morning, his partner gives him feedback that it was really nice to just hang out and be together last night. Usually, after dinner, Andres goes right back into his home office and works as late as he can bear. Often, his partner is already sound asleep when he shuts down. He appreciates the unsolicited feedback and that his partner noticed he took the night off.

The next night – Thursday – Andres is back to his old routines. But something is different this time. He notices how grumpy he is to go back to work after dinner. He's had a taste of what it was like to take the night off and relax. Even more noteworthy, the next morning – after working until 10:30 pm – he wakes up groggy and grumpy once again. He drags himself to the coffee machine and looks with dread at the full calendar on his phone. His partner makes a sarcastic comment later that day, asking if he even went to bed since he was still working at bedtime and was already back at work by the time his partner awoke. Andres winces at the comment but perceives it as important feedback about the impact of his choices.

In this example, Andres experiments with his behavior, pays careful attention to notice and reflect on what he experiences, and gets feedback from someone who also notices his behavior and whose opinion he cares about deeply. Andres has his work cut out for him. He has dipped a toe into advancing toward his goal of a more balanced lifestyle but will have to rely extensively on self-regulation and self-control to shift his long-held and often reinforced work habits. Having an added layer of support and accountability can help. Research has shown that when individuals work with a coach, they are significantly more likely to achieve their goals.[17] Coaching can provide the structure, time, and space to stop and reflect on goals and behavior, and to make intentional choices about behavior change. Additionally, many clients feel a sense of responsibility and accountability to their coach to show that they are making an effort and doing the work to make meaningful progress. As we mentioned before, behavior change is hard, particularly when we go it alone. Having an objective partner, sounding board, or accountability buddy, such as a coach, friend, colleague, family member, or therapist, can set us up for a greater likelihood of success, particularly if they are willing to do the brave work of sharing candid feedback and observations.

Habits: the path of least resistance

As we mentioned in Chapter 2, our brains favor ease and efficiency. Making deliberate choices about our behaviors and thinking deeply about decisions is neither easy nor efficient! Think about a typical day in your life. Imagine how overwhelmed and exhausted you would feel if you had to make a deliberate choice about every single thing you did throughout the day – from the moment you wake up to the moment you go to bed. Research has shown that roughly 45% of our behaviors on any given day are made up entirely of habits,[18] as opposed to deliberate choices. Relying on habits allows us to allocate our decision-making and cognitive energy to decisions and behaviors that warrant more attention. For example, if you have had the same morning routine for 12 years, it probably unfolds each day without you even noticing. But as soon as something unusual or demanding of your attention occurs, your awareness shifts. The electricity goes out, your partner cuts their hand while slicing a bagel, you have a 5 am conference call. Suddenly, with these novel situations, your habitual morning routine is disrupted, and you have to make more intentional choices about where you direct your energy and attention.

Our habits form through a sequence of steps. First, we experience a cue or trigger that motivates some kind of behavior. Then, the behavior is rewarded or reinforced. We learn that this behavior leads to a positive outcome, so we are likely to repeat it. With repetition, we associate the behavior with, first, the cue, and second, the reward. For example, the clock strikes 5 pm on Friday. You close your laptop, pack up your things, and – doesn't an ice-cold beer sound great right now? You go to the fridge, crack open a cold one, and feel the work week melt away and the calm possibility of the weekend come into focus. Next thing you know, you've been cracking open that cold beer every Friday at 5 pm for years – it's become habitual. You find yourself in that groove that we talked about earlier. In this example, the cue is the clock striking 5 pm and you packing up your things. The behavior is cracking open a beer, and the reward is that sense of calm completion you feel wash over you. Here's another example. It's 10 pm, and you're getting tired. You get ready for bed and hop under the covers. You grab your phone and start scrolling through social media, commenting on or liking your friends' posts. Next thing you know, 45 minutes have flown by. What happened? In this example, the cue was getting in bed and reaching for your phone. The behavior is scrolling through social media, and the reward is the emotions you generate by commenting on and liking your friends' posts (and perhaps seeing some likes and comments on your own).

Now you're tired of mindlessly scrolling through social media and wasting time every night when you could be getting more sleep. How do you intercept the habit? In his book *The Power of Habit*,[19] author and journalist Charles Duhigg explains that we must get under the surface of the real benefits we are getting from the habit and find ways to break the cue-behavior-reward pattern. In our social media example, you could change the cue-behavior cycle by leaving your phone on the kitchen counter at night and using an old-school alarm clock rather than your phone's alarm. Or you could dig deep on what you're REALLY getting out of the social media scrolling. Perhaps it's a feeling of connection with people you care about, or a feeling of external validation when others like or comment on your posts. To change the habit, you'll want to find connection or validation elsewhere, such as through a phone call with a close friend or writing a few thank-you notes to people you care about (real mail!). These alternative behaviors will give you the same benefit (reward) of connecting with others, while allowing you to let go of your social media scrolling habit.

Noticing, pausing, and making intentional choices are essential for adjusting habits. The key to creating new habits or abandoning or changing habits that no longer serve us starts with becoming aware of those habits. You can't intentionally change behaviors that you don't see or are not aware of. The skill of noticing is essential for becoming more consciously aware of habits that drive our behavior each day. Once we become aware of those habits, we can pause to identify the three elements mentioned above: the cue, the actual behavior, and the reward that is reinforcing that behavior. Pausing also provides the time and space to stop and make a conscious choice about a different behavior we want to try instead.

Experience it yourself

Take a moment to identify a few habits that drive your behavior on a regular basis:

1. _____

2. _____

3. _____

4. _____

5. _____

Pick one of those habits and break it down into its components.

What is the cue or trigger?

_____

_____

_____

What is the actual behavior?

_____

_____

_____

What reward do you get from that behavior? Dig deep here – what is it really reinforcing for you?

_____

_____

_____

> *How well is this habit working for you? What do you want to keep doing or change? Why?*
>
> _____
>
> _____
>
> _____

Conclusion

All day, every day you experience emotions and cognitions that drive and are impacted by your behavior and the choices you make. And you have more choice than you realize. Our goals can help keep us pointed in the right direction, and we all possess the capacity and discipline to pause, notice, and choose a different behavior in support of our goals. It's simple and effective, even if it isn't easy. Over time we create new habits and new typical ways of being for ourselves that are more aligned to who we want to be and the effect we want to have on others and the world around us.

In the next section we shift from focusing on you, to exploring you in relation to other people. We don't live in a vacuum, and much of life occurs alongside other people. Everything you have learned about yourself and how your brain works applies to others too. That can be easy to forget sometimes. We over-index on what we see people doing and make inferences about their motivations and intentions, even though we might be entirely off base. Come with us now as we zoom out to talk about you in relation to other people, and how you can leverage your knowledge of your own emotions, cognition, and behavior to have more effective interactions with others.

Chapter 3 Key idea

Our reactions are not fixed – we can learn techniques to help us perceive and respond to the world in ways that better serve us. Having greater clarity around your goals can help you set intentions, harness your motivation, and align your choices to better achieve them.

Want to learn more? Check out

One of our favorite tools to break goals down into manageable steps and become more aware of our daily habits is the **Habit Tracker** tool from

Appointed, maker of notebooks, productivity tools, and other great work supplies. Great for those of you who prefer good old-fashioned paper over apps and online tools. Check out appointed.co for more. There are also a variety of apps that you can use for tracking goals and habits.

Recommended reading

Behave and *Why zebras don't get ulcers*, both by Robert Sapolsky

On the self-regulation of behavior by Charles S. Carver & Michael F. Scheier

The power of habit by Charles Duhigg

Notes

1 Your parasympathetic nervous system, also known as "rest and digest," controls your ability to relax and slow down. Your sympathetic nervous system does the opposite – it gets you ready for fight or flight when you perceive a threat or danger.

2 Sapolsky, R. M. (2017). *Behave: The biology of humans at our best and worst*. New York, NY: Penguin Press.

3 Carver, C. S., & Scheier, M. F. (1996). Self-regulation and its failures. *Psychological Inquiry*, 7(1), 32–40. https://doi.org/10.1207/s15327965pli0701_6

4 Klein, K., & Boals, A. (2001). Expressive writing can increase working memory capacity. *Journal of Experimental Psychology: General*, 130(3), 520–533. https://doi.org/10.1037/0096-3445.130.3.520

5 Karpicke, J. (2012). Retrieval-based learning: Active retrieval promotes meaningful learning. *Current Directions in Psychological Science*, 21(3), 157–163. https://doi.org/10.1177/0963721412443552

    Roediger, H. L. (2000). Why retrieval is the key process in understanding human memory. In E. Tulving (Ed.), *Memory, consciousness, and the brain: The Tallinn conference* (pp. 52–75). Philadelphia, PA: Psychology Press.

6 Bargh, J. (2017). *Before you know it: The unconscious reasons we do what we do*. New York, NY: Touchstone.

7 Ford, M., & Smith, P. (2020). *Motivating self and others: Thriving with social purpose, life meaning, and the pursuit of core personal goals*. Cambridge University Press. https://doi.org/10.1017/9781108869164

8 Immordino-Yang, M. H. (2016). Emotion, sociality, and the brain's default mode network: Insights for educational practice and policy. *Policy Insights from the Behavioral and Brain Sciences*, 3(2), 211–219. https://doi.org/10.1177/2372732216656869

 9 Rothman, A. J., Baldwin, A. S., Hertel, A. W., & Fuglestad, P. T. (2011). Self-regulation and behavior change: Disentangling behavioral initiation and behavioral maintenance. In K. D. Vohs & R. F. Baumeister (Eds.), *Handbook of self-regulation: Research, theory, and applications* (pp. 106–122). New York: Guilford Press.

10 Baumeister, R. F., Schmeichel, B. J., & Vohs, K. D. (2007). Self-regulation and the executive function: The self as controlling agent. In A. W. Kruglanski & E. T. Higgins (Eds.), *Social psychology: Handbook of basic principles* (2nd ed., pp. 516–539). New York, NY: Guilford.

11 International Coaching Federation. (2021). *ICF core competencies.* https://coach federation.org/core-competencies

12 Gollwitzer, P. M. (1999). Implementation intentions: Strong effects of simple plans. *American Psychologist, 54*(7), 493–503. https://doi.org/10.1037/0003-066X. 54.7.493

13 Carver & Scheier. (1996). Self-regulation, 32–40.

14 For deeper reading on the topic of competing goals and tools to identify and overcome them, see *Immunity to Change* by Lisa Lahey and Robert Kegan.

15 Jones, N. P., Papadakis, A. A., Orr, C. A., & Strauman, T. J. (2013). Cognitive processes in response to goal failure: A study of ruminative thought and its affective consequences. *Journal of Social and Clinical Psychology, 32*(5), 482–503. https://doi.org/10.1521/jscp.2013.32.5.482

16 Amabile, T., & Kramer, S. (2011). *The progress principle: Using small wins to ignite joy, engagement, and creativity at work.* Boston, MA: Harvard Business Press.

17 Grant, A. M., Curtayne, L., & Burton, G. (2009). Executive coaching enhances goal attainment, resilience and workplace well-being: A randomised controlled study. *The Journal of Positive Psychology, 4*(5), 396–407. https://doi.org/10.1080/17439760902992456

18 Neal, D. T., Wood, W., Wu, M., & Kurlander, D. (2011). The pull of the past: When do habits persist despite conflict with motives? *Personality and Social Psychology Bulletin, 37*(11), 1428–1437. https://doi.org/10.1177/0146167211419863

19 Duhigg, C. (2012). *The power of habit: Why we do what we do in life and business.* New York: Random House.

Part 2

Your coaching skills

Part 1 of this book introduced some concepts and frameworks, grounded in research, to help you think more deliberately about what's happening under the surface that is influencing what is showing up above the waterline. As we introduced those concepts, we included some reflective exercises and tools that you can use to influence your own thoughts, feelings, and actions. In Part 2, we'll introduce coaching skills that you can use to not only influence your internal world but also to influence your relationships and the world around you. We begin with 1:1 relationships in Chapter 4 and then progress to how coaching skills can be applied to 1:many relationships such as groups and teams in Chapter 5. In doing so, we explore both how the psychological principles described in Part 1 give rise to coaching skills and tools, and how those psychological principles shift as people interact with one another. Part 2 will give you a better sense of how you can apply a coaching mindset and skills to more effectively influence the actions of others or assist others in doing so.

DOI: 10.4324/9781003166917-5

4
Using your coaching skills 1:1

Questions we'll answer in this chapter:

1. Are we finally going to talk about coaching skills?
2. How does what we learned about ourselves apply to our interactions with others?
3. What makes coaching distinct from other types of conversations?

I need you to reset table 46 NOW. Casey looked at the text on their phone and immediately felt both puzzled and hijacked. "What is the deal? And who do you think you are, talking to me like that?" Casey thought as they considered the message. Casey is the daytime manager of an established and beloved Michelin-starred restaurant. They love their job and care deeply about service and creating wonderful experiences for guests. Still feeling annoyed and confused, Casey hustles to the garden dining room and grabs a few staff members on the way to get table 46 cleared and reset. Twenty minutes later, Casey runs into Stella, the restaurant general manager and sender of the cryptic text. Stella appears tense and frazzled. Casey thinks, "Oh, geez, now what?" but feigns a smile to Stella. They have a full book of reservations on this Friday afternoon going into a long weekend, so there's no time for squabbles. As the afternoon unfolds Casey ruminates on the text from Stella and starts to concoct stories about Stella's intentions. By the time lunch service wraps up, Casey has decided it might be time to look around on the job market. "Why would I want to work somewhere where I feel disrespected and ordered around like this?" After a meeting with the evening leadership crew, Stella asks Casey for a word. "Oh, here it comes," Casey mutters under their breath.

Stella pulls Casey to the side and says quietly, "I'm so sorry that I was tense and distracted earlier. Thank you for taking care of table 46 so quickly! We

DOI: 10.4324/9781003166917-6

found out with 15 minutes notice that a team from the *LA Times* food section was coming in for lunch! Their last write-up about us was a little critical, and I wanted to make sure we were ready for them this time." Instantly, Casey feels mortified after spending the entire afternoon in a downward spiral of emotions, judgments, and making plans to move on! All from one little text and making assumptions about Stella's demeanor when they ran into each other before service began. Casey reassures Stella everything was okay and asks about the *LA Times* team's experience. Casey half listens to Stella, but finds that they are distracted by an inner monologue of thoughts like "OMG, you are so emotional! You jumped to conclusions so fast! What is wrong with you?!" On their walk home from the restaurant, Casey plays back the day in their mind, wondering how they could have handled the situation differently. If we could see inside Casey's head, we would see their thoughts unfold: "Instead of jumping to these conclusions and getting bent out of shape by Stella's text, I should have just written back and asked what was going on. I trust Stella, and we have a great working relationship. I should have known something was going on after that text and when I saw her looking tense. She's usually so calm and kind. I can't believe I took it personally and thought it was something about me. Next time, I'm going to ask. I'm going to take care of the work that needs to be addressed, but try to understand why, what's going on. I also wish I had asked Stella if she was okay rather than giving her that fake smile when I ran into her. I can't believe I did that!"

When was the last time you had an experience like Casey's? You jumped to conclusions, making assumptions about someone's words or behavior. You created a cascade of imagined thoughts, feelings, and actions without pausing to understand what's really going on. Sound familiar? If so, read on.

1+1=3

In Chapters 1–3, we offered a window into a few of the influences and drivers of our thoughts, feelings, and behavior. So much more is happening beneath the surface to shape our own and others' observable behaviors. This is often depicted as an iceberg, with what we see above the surface (e.g., behaviors) being just a small fraction of the picture. At any given moment, we experience a multitude of thoughts, feelings, observations, and impulses, much of which we're not consciously aware of. We could write an entire book (and many, many people have!) on just one layer of the iceberg to understand its complexity.

Behavior

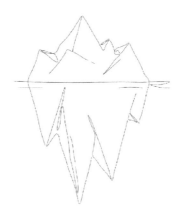

Emotions, Values and Beliefs

The complexity doesn't end there. We don't live our lives in isolation. As other people enter the mix, complexity grows, and their icebergs collide with our own. Just as every person is unique, every relationship is unique. Relationships are not just my iceberg plus yours; there's an interaction between two people that creates a fundamentally new phenomenon.[1] With all that complexity, it's amazing that we get along as well as we do! And yet, there are endless opportunities for misunderstandings, conflict, and discontent. Many of the most important relationships in our lives are 1:1 (dyadic). You and your partner, mother, father, manager, neighbor, best friend, teacher, child, and so on. In this chapter we'll talk about how you can bring a coaching mindset and skill set to those relationships and to each interaction to be more effective and bring out the best in others, first in 1:1 settings and then with groups and teams in Chapter 5.

Up until now, we've primarily discussed concepts through the lens of an individual. You perceive someone else's behavior and go through a wide array of fast and slow processing to interpret that behavior and respond. The story doesn't end there. Your behavior also impacts others. Behavior can create a chain reaction; one that might take us down a path we don't want to be on. As we described in Chapter 3, pause practices can be a powerful way to break the chain – particularly because the only behavior you can control is your own (and you can't necessarily count on the other person having a pause practice). Often, 1:1 interactions come to life through dialogue. This is where your coaching skill set can be your superpower. Now that you have the foundational concepts of the self, we'll dive into core coaching skills that you'll then see how to apply in every aspect of life throughout the rest of this book. Yes, we are finally getting to coaching skills now.

In Chapter 1, we introduced professional coaching as "partnering with clients in a thought-provoking and creative process that inspires them to maximize their personal and professional potential."[2] We also noted that this book was not written for professional coaches. Instead, we draw from the core coaching skill set professional coaches use and that anyone can develop and apply to improve their own emotional regulation, thought patterns, behaviors, and interactions with others. You can think of this as us drawing a distinction between "coach" as a noun (e.g., a professional coach or person who is playing the role of a coach) and "coach" as a verb – the core skills that coaches use in their practice, and that you can also use to have more effective interactions with others. In this book, we focus on coach as a verb.

Mindset is everything

Think about the last time you were offended in an interaction. Was it the actual words? Was it the tone? Was it your memory of your previous interaction with that person? The mindset we bring to a conversation impacts not only the way we understand the world around us, but also the way we are understood. One example of mindset that you might have encountered is the idea of *growth mindset*.[3] Growth mindset is the belief that you can develop your abilities through hard work, focus, and effort rather than the belief that your abilities are innate or "fixed" (fixed mindset). Research has consistently demonstrated that this difference in how people perceive ability has big implications for how they approach tasks, deal with setbacks, and as a result, the kind of outcomes they achieve.

Let's look at an example of how this might show up in practice. Two of Shonna's closest childhood friends were naturally gifted artists. They loved to draw and would spend hours practicing – tracing, practicing freehand, and developing new cartoon characters. Shonna, in contrast, gravitated toward reading and science. For years, whenever Shonna and her friends worked on group projects, she would rely on them for the artistic aspects of the project while she took on the things that required research, writing, or organization. As a result, while her friends dedicated hours, months, and eventually years to their craft, Shonna avoided anything artistic because, in her words, "*I wasn't good at it.*" Whose artistic skills do you imagine improved over that time? Some activities certainly come more naturally to each of us, but the mindset you have about those differences influences the story you tell yourself about your capabilities and ultimately what you do about it. As an adult, Shonna has intentionally shifted the stories she tells herself and as a result, now loves to draw, paint, and sculpt.

We often find that realizing you can choose your mindset is mind-blowing to some people. They haven't considered the degree of choice that they have in how they decide to "show up," or frame or interpret their experiences. In our class at Georgetown University, we start by encouraging our students to take a beginner's mindset, where they approach their experiences with curiosity and wonder, rather than assuming they already know the answers.

The mindset that you choose to adopt in any given situation will influence how you experience that situation. For example, let's say you hate networking events and typically enter them with a mindset of discomfort and feeling like networking is sleezy – like you are using people to get ahead. Instead, you could intentionally choose a mindset of curiosity, which will enable you to naturally be more interested in the people you are meeting and the experience that you are having. You can probably imagine that you'll have a more enjoyable time at the event if you go in with openness and curiosity rather than feeling closed off and having labeled the event as sleezy.

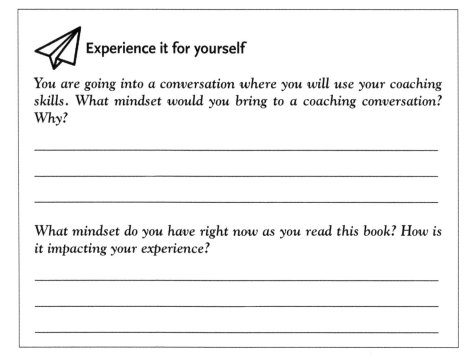

Experience it for yourself

You are going into a conversation where you will use your coaching skills. What mindset would you bring to a coaching conversation? Why?

_____

_____

_____

What mindset do you have right now as you read this book? How is it impacting your experience?

_____

_____

_____

Having a growth or fixed mindset impacts how you learn and deal with challenges. There are many other aspects of mindset that impact our interactions with others every day. The International Coaching Federation recently did an extensive study[4] to update their list of competencies required to be an effective coach (for more on the competencies visit the International Coaching Federation Website). One of the competencies identified was *Embodies a Coaching Mindset*, which entails "developing and maintaining a mindset that is open, curious, flexible and client-centered." One of the most important aspects of the coaching mindset is to be truly curious about the other person, what they are experiencing, and how they make sense of the world. That curiosity must be followed by openness and non-judgment. When you use your coaching skills, you want the person you are talking with to feel comfortable being open, honest, and authentic. You want them to feel as if they are being accepted, and not judged or evaluated, for sharing their honest thoughts and feelings. To create this environment, you must start with your mindset. The mindset that you bring to the conversation lays the foundation for everything that you do and say. These foundational ways of approaching a conversation are below the waterline in the iceberg model but have a massive impact on what shows up above. We like to think of these as being a new kind of CON artist (curious, open, non-judgmental).

A new kind of CON artist

As we've noted throughout the book, people are social creatures who evolved to depend on one another for survival in an environment filled with creatures far larger, stronger, and faster than we were. This means that feelings of judgment trigger primal insecurity and fear related to exclusion from the group. Being excluded or rejected from the group was a matter of survival. Even though everyday threats to our survival are less likely in the modern world, our brains still respond to *imagined* threats (judgment, rejection, exclusion) in the same way they would respond to those real threats (lions, tigers, and bears!). Coaching, particularly with the intention of development, requires that the other person feels safe so that they can be vulnerable, receptive to challenge, and confident in their ability to grow.

✈ Experience it yourself

Reflect on a time when you felt judged. What was the situation? What caused you to feel like you were being judged?

_____

_____

_____

What was the impact? How did you respond?

_____

_____

_____

Now, reflect on a time when you felt safe and accepted. What was the situation? What caused you to feel like you were accepted?

_____

_____

_____

What was the impact? How did you respond?

_____

_____

_____

These concepts also highlight the intersection between coaching and diversity, inclusion, and belonging. Those ideas are fundamentally intertwined because much of coaching is built on the foundation that to be in service of and with others, you need to show up in a way that enables them to feel seen and heard. When we feel like we don't belong, we are less likely to take risks, and we might deliberately try to stay off the radar, which means we are less likely to get noticed or have opportunities shared with us that enable us to achieve our goals and have significant impact. We censor ourselves, which causes us to lose the potential for beneficial relationships and opportunities for growth and development. In contrast, when people feel like they belong, they are more willing to offer diverse perspectives, take in the perspectives of others, and show up as their full, authentic selves. The Coaching Mindset competency highlights the importance of self-awareness, reflection, curiosity, emotional regulation, and humility – asking for help, continuously learning, and being open to and aware of the influence of context and culture on ourselves and others.

Those soft skills sure are hard

Although you don't have to be a coach to use coaching *skills*, we still believe it can be helpful to understand the competencies that define professional coaching and consider how these behaviors can be applied in our day-to-day lives. The International Coaching Federation (ICF)[5] outlines eight core competencies (grouped into four domains) for coaches, each of which includes several specific behaviors to bring that competency to life. These competencies are based on rigorous research with more than 1300 coaches across the globe. The purpose is to provide consistency and clarity on the skills and behaviors that contribute to effective coaching. For our purposes, we focus on four of those eight competencies that we believe are most relevant to the coaching skill set: Establishes and Maintains Agreements, Listens Actively, Evokes Awareness, and Facilitates Client Growth. If you are interested in learning more about the remaining four competencies (which we deem most appropriate for professional coaches), visit the International Coach Federation website.[6] Let's take a look at the first of our four focal competencies: Establishing and Maintaining Agreements.

Setting the destination in your conversational GPS

Coaching conversations are not just interesting conversations. They are purposeful. They have an intended outcome with some structure – a

beginning, middle, and end. The beginning of the conversation includes an agreement. The agreement establishes the focus of the conversation and what will be accomplished. Agreements provide an important foundation for the conversation. They give us guideposts for the conversation and a way to evaluate success and ensure it's not an aimless chit-chat. Knowing what the other person wants to achieve in the conversation ensures that the coach can offer observations and new ways of seeing that might help the other person achieve that outcome. Our day-to-day interactions often begin and end without clear agreement on the purpose of the conversation and what success looks like. We set recurring meetings, often without stopping to evaluate whether they are still a good use of time. We call a friend to chat about a problem without clarifying whether what we need is an ear or advice.

In a formal coaching relationship, the coach and client typically develop a formal agreement, often codified in a coaching contract, regarding the nature of the relationship, the client's goals, and how they will work together. This creates stronger alignment between the coach and client, which reduces the likelihood of unmet expectations and sets a strong foundation for direct feedback throughout the relationship. For most of us, we'll find ourselves incorporating coaching skills into our toolkit outside the confines of a professional coaching relationship. "Coach" might be one of many hats you find yourself wearing in any given relationship, perhaps in addition to manager, trusted advisor, mentor, or friend.

Let's take the role of a parent. We'll use Shonna as our example because she has three daughters. Shonna has both intentionally and unintentionally incorporated coaching into the tools she uses in her relationships with her daughters since being trained as a coach. There are many other roles she plays and tools she uses, however. When one of her daughters comes to her feeling frustrated or upset, how does she know which tool to use? Shonna could give her daughter advice (her mentor hat), teach her (her teacher or trainer hat), tell her what to do (her parent or supervisor hat), or listen and ask her questions to help her further explore her thoughts and feelings (her coach hat). What's the best way to respond? Arguably, the best way for Shonna to respond is the way that most closely aligns with what her daughter wants or believes she needs in that moment. The first step to forming an agreement on the conversation would be to ask her daughter. We often skip this step. We typically assume, even if unconsciously, what will be most helpful and dive right in. That might not align with what help looks like to Shonna's daughter in that situation. She may be looking for someone to listen and validate, while Shonna is anxious to give advice and problem solve (how many times have you been here: you just want someone to listen, but they are trying to give advice and solve your problem!). Coming to an agreement can help identify and close that gap.

Agreements can be even more important in multifaceted work relationships. Take the role of a manager. Expectations of modern managers often include manager as coach, supervisor, and mentor. In addition, it is not uncommon for friendships to develop (we won't even get into family businesses). Ensuring that both parties are aligned on the context of the discussion can increase trust and safety. Further, agreements can be valuable but often absent from many other aspects of corporate life. For example, take meetings. An agenda is an example of an agreement. In his great book, *The Surprising Science of Meetings*,[7] industrial-organizational psychologist Steven Rogelberg notes that having a clear agenda that others in the meeting have had some say in can lead to a more effective meeting and time better spent. Simple questions can be some of the most powerful in framing the purpose of a meeting. What is it we're here to discuss? What does success look like? Once we have an upfront agreement, we've created the necessary foundation for others to commit. We create a way to evaluate goal attainment and success of the engagement. Although being explicit about an agreement can feel constraining, it opens the potential to pursue alternative ways of achieving the desired outcome. In our work with our clients, we frequently find that disappointment is a result of unmet (and unstated) expectations rather than broken promises. Discipline around agreements can clarify expectations and reduce the likelihood of disappointment.

✈ **Experience it yourself**

In your next meeting, notice the presence or absence of clear agreements. Consider the following questions:

What is the agreement?

_____

_____

_____

What are the measures of success?

_____

_____

_____

Why is the agreement important/meaningful?

_____

_____

_____

Is the agreement clear? What would make it clearer?

_____

_____

_____

Two ears, one mouth

We asserted that the desires to feel seen and heard are deeply innate human needs that have roots in our basic survival as a species. In our experience, it's relatively rare that people feel heard in their day-to-day lives. It's a seemingly simple activity. Yet, when you start to pay attention to your own listening, and the listening of others, you might find that we engage in and are the recipients of far less real listening than you might imagine. Listening requires focused attention. Focused attention is effortful. As we described in Chapter 2, a lot of data are coming at us at any given time and there are countless demands on our attention. Even now, things might be pulling you away from the words on this page. It might be sounds or goings-on in your environment. It could be your inner monologue, your to-do list, what you're going to have for dinner, or that thing that happened last week that keeps creeping into your thoughts. The same thing happens when we're engaging in conversation with others. When you listen to truly understand the other person, you are shifting into a depth of listening that requires practice. This idea is referred to as "levels of listening."

Internal listening (level 1)

In our coach training we learned about three levels of listening,[8] which we refer back to regularly in our own coaching work and in our class. In level 1 listening, despite being in conversation with someone else, our attention is on ourselves. If you've ever found yourself interrupting another person or anxiously waiting for them to complete their sentence so that you don't forget what you were going to say, you have practiced level 1 listening. When someone shares instructions with you and you listen closely with your own follow-up actions in mind, you're listening at level 1. If a friend tells you about their vacation to Key West and you say, "I love Key West!" you are practicing level 1 listening. We all practice level 1 listening or *internal listening* every single day. In fact, we likely spend most of our time listening at this level. There is nothing inherently bad or wrong with level 1 listening. Despite the inferred hierarchy of levels 1, 2, and 3, no one level is superior to the other. Each level of listening serves its own purpose. Listening at level 1 is efficient and helps us identify information that is relevant to us. It can also help us find things we share with others (we both love Key West!). At other times we may benefit from stepping back to notice our own excitement about and preoccupation with our great response and the idea we want to communicate when given the chance; we are focused on ourselves, not the other person.

Focused listening (level 2)

When we shift our attention from ourselves to the other person, we move to level 2 listening (*focused listening*). When we listen at level 2, we give our undivided attention to the person we're listening to. We listen closely to really understand what they are saying. We pay careful attention to their words, and pick up on the tone of their voice, the pace of their speech, their facial expressions and body language. We are listening not only with our ears, but also with our eyes and our full attention. Listening at this level means that we are taking in and processing significantly more data, which requires more of our energy and cognitive resources. Really listening at level 2 requires us to quiet our inner monologue, eliminate distractions like phone or computer notifications, and be fully present with the other person.

Global listening (level 3)

When we tune in even more and listen at level 3 (*global listening*), we can pick up on what is said, how it is said (body language, tone), and what is *not* said. We are using all our resources – ears, eyes, attention, mind, and hearts – to listen to the whole person. Some coaches like to say that level 3 listening also draws on their intuition; they pick up on nuances, feelings, and impressions from the other person that are very subtle. This level of listening also requires an awareness of the context – what is happening in the room or around this person you are listening to so deeply – which can provide additional useful data. When you have the experience of being listened to at level 3, you feel seen and heard in ways you may be unaccustomed to.

During the widespread shift to virtual work in 2020, we heard questions and comments from colleagues, clients, and students about the difficulty of connecting deeply with others when you cannot be together in person. Listening at level 3 is still possible in a virtual environment, but it requires truly focused attention, given the vast array of distractions coming from technology or being in different environments. It requires a certain level of adjustment and getting comfortable engaging virtually, since most of us have spent most of our lives being "in person" with others. It also requires deliberate communication to bridge any gaps through cyberspace. For example, we don't always see exactly what is happening in our companion's physical space when we are on video calls. Imagine you are having an in-depth and challenging feedback conversation using a video conferencing platform. You have done all that you can to control your environment – turning off email notifications on your computer, silencing your phone, clearing your desk. But suddenly construction noise outside your window pulls a fragment of your attention away. If the person you're speaking to can't hear that construction noise, they may notice the blip in your attention and wonder if you are present and listening. However, if you were in the same physical room together, you would both hear the construction noise and there would be no mystery about what's pulled away your attention. This is where your skill of *naming* can be so powerful. Simply letting the other person know what you are experiencing minimizes any doubts they have about you being fully present. When they know they can attribute the pause in your attention to noise, and not to them being dull or droning on, you'll both be able to return to presence and regain focus in the virtual environment. Research has shown that when we speak to undistracted, attentive listeners, we tend to feel less anxious, be more self-aware, and have greater clarity about our own attitudes.[9] We are also motivated to share *more* with people who are attentive and undistracted!

Though this may seem counterintuitive, we find that you can get just as much, if not more data when having a deep and focused conversation on the phone, with no video. Although you may miss out on the opportunity to notice facial expressions and body language, being on the phone can move you to listen with a tremendous level of depth and intention, to the point that you pick up on subtle data and cues like the other person's pauses, how deeply they breathe, where there's a quiver in their voice or where their pace changes.

Levels of Listening

Level 1
(Internal Listening)
Listening with yourself in mind

Level 2
(Focused Listening)
Listening attentively for words, tone, expressions

Level 3
(Global listening)
Listening with attention and heart to the whole person

Let's return to Casey's story. They sensed that Stella was tense – even frazzled. Casey didn't respond to that data with focused attention. They didn't get curious or ask questions. They didn't ask about what wasn't being said. Casey was focused on the conversation going on within themselves rather than with Stella or within Stella. That doesn't make Casey a selfish person. It's natural to see things through your own lens. Learning to be more aware of how you're listening and hone your skills at listening more deeply can create more choices. Listening deeply to another person is a gift. If Casey had shifted into level 2 listening when they ran into Stella, rather than feigning a smile, Stella might have felt supported. She might have felt less stressed, knowing that she had someone in her corner. She could have remembered that she's not alone – an entire team of people is invested in making the restaurant successful. Who knows? That might have even helped Stella deliver a five-star experience for the critic. Stella might have seen Casey in a new light – as a partner rather than a direct report. Listening is a seemingly basic skill with unlimited potential.

Although listening seems straightforward, there's no shortage of things that can get in the way of doing it well. It helps to be intentional about setting the environment up for attentive listening. You won't be set up for success if you're trying to listen at level 3 but your phone keeps buzzing with notifications. In Casey's situation, multiple things might have gotten in the way of their listening more deeply. They might have had tables to greet or food to deliver. One of the biggest barriers was story – the story Casey told themself about a text message. We're always telling stories. This is another place where awareness can open up choices. The only fact in Casey's story was that Stella sent a text message telling them to set the table now. Everything else – the entire path that led Casey down the path to ultimately thinking about leaving their job – was a story. As you start to be able to distinguish fact from fiction, you give yourself more options regarding the story you choose to tell. In the context of 1:1 relationships, choosing a story that assumes positive intent is more likely to create the space for you to get curious, understand the other person's perspective, clarify misunderstandings, and ultimately build a stronger foundation of trust.

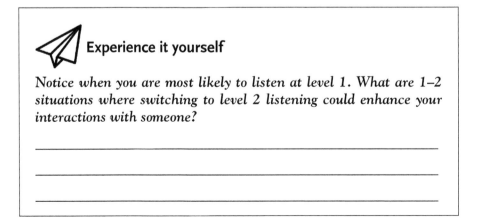

Experience it yourself

Notice when you are most likely to listen at level 1. What are 1–2 situations where switching to level 2 listening could enhance your interactions with someone?

_____

_____

_____

It's the questions that enlighten us

In Chapters 2 and 3 we talked about what's going on beneath the surface that can cause us to feel stuck. It might be that we're hooked by our emotions or are only seeing one path forward. We suggested that pausing to create space, breathe, and ask a question of yourself (e.g., "how could I be wrong?") can be a powerful tool in getting yourself "unstuck." We're often stuck in relation to others, or we're witness to another person being stuck. Perhaps you have had this experience, where you can see another person struggling with a decision or "getting in their own way." You can see that they are stuck, and perhaps even WHY they are stuck, but it's not always easy to recognize it in ourselves or see clearly what we need to do to get unstuck. This is where another coaching competency comes into play: Evoking awareness.

Coaches evoke awareness in others by using a range of tools including silence, metaphor, analogy, and so on. But the most well-known coaching tool is the *question*. Questions play multiple roles in coaching. First, asking questions is key to trust and relationship building, communication, and task performance. Research has shown that asking questions even increases how likable you are![10] Questions empower the other person and signal that you're willing to listen. The relationship between two people, whether it be coach and client, manager and employee, or two team members, is one of the biggest predictors of important outcomes.[11] The real power of questions is not the listener (aka question-asker) getting information, but in helping the other person think through their answer to the question, share their perspective, hear their words out loud (rather than just in their head), and feel heard.

Beyond setting the foundation for the relationship, questions change the trajectory of a conversation in other ways. They surface underlying assumptions and stimulate creativity and fresh thinking. Questions are a foundational part of coaching because they help stimulate awareness and reflection. Asking a question causes the other person to think and engage more, which improves learning.[12] The right questions also help to build trust and strengthen relationships and bonds. A powerful question can open the door to change and lead us into the future.

The real value of asking questions lies in raising awareness for the other person and ensuring that they own the solution to their challenge. A common Chinese proverb that we mentioned earlier illustrates this value: "You give a poor man a fish and you feed him for a day. You teach him to fish and you give him an occupation that will feed him for a lifetime." For most people,

> ✈ **Experience it yourself**
>
> *Think of a time when someone asked you a helpful or curious question. What was the impact of that experience for you?*
>
> _____
>
> _____
>
> _____

when we encounter another person with a problem, we often feel a strong desire to fix it. We want to help them. We want to feel useful. We're more comfortable with actions than we are with feelings. Ultimately, this leads to giving advice. In his book, *The Advice Trap*,[13] Michael Bungay-Stanier explores our impulse to chime in with ideas, suggestions, and advice under the guise of helping the other person. But the problem is, no matter how well we think we know them or the situation, or understand what they need or want, we can never really know. Our perspective on the situation is inherently clouded by our own lens and interpretation. Not to mention, people generally don't like to be told what to do. Instead of offering advice or telling people what they "should" do, we can be a much better friend, colleague, and steward of their success by asking a question that helps them arrive at the answer on their own. By coming to their own solution, not only will the solution be more relevant for them (because they know more than you!), but they will also feel more ownership and motivation to do something with it. This notion is the heart of coaching: A deep belief that people are creative, resourceful, and whole. They can solve their own problems and will be more committed to the solutions that they come up with than any we could ever provide. And the best part is, they learn by doing, developing their problem-solving muscles through the process.

> Coaching is not about telling people what to do,
> but about facilitating their process of discovery

Not all questions are equally likely to catalyze learning and lead us into the future. Sometimes our questions are just statements of advice with a question mark at the end. "Why" questions tend to engender defensiveness.

Rhetorical questions and closed or yes/no questions don't leave much space for creativity, exploration, and reflection. You might have noticed that we've embedded questions in the exercises throughout this book that mimic a coaching dialogue. We did this intentionally to model what this might look like in practice and to further your learning. Questions facilitate reflection, which facilitates active processing of information, increasing long-term memory storage and mastery.[14]

We asked friends, colleagues, and students to share a few of their favorite questions. Here are some highlights from their contributions:

- What does success look like?
- What do you want to figure out?
- What's really at the heart of this?
- What would you change if you had a magic wand?
- If everything fell perfectly into place, what would that look like?
- What else? (inspired by Michael Bungay-Stanier's great AWE question – "And what else?")
- I'm curious about . . .
- Tell me more about . . .
- If our roles were reversed, what would you tell me to do?
- What do you really want?
- What is the hardest part of this for you?

You can practice asking questions that have a greater likelihood of being "powerful." This begins with your mindset – being curious and asking the questions you do not know the answer to. "What" and "how" questions tend to be the most powerful. When you first start to notice and to practice, you might find yourself asking long, complex, and even meandering questions. Practice asking simple questions. Let your curiosity guide you, but only ask one question at a time. If you ask a question and the other person is silent, don't panic! Silence is often a sign that your question was powerful. It made the other person stop and think. Rather than rushing in to ask it another way or explain yourself, stay quiet. Learning to be comfortable with silence is an important skill to complement questions. If you're uncomfortable with silence, reframe it as creating space for the other person. If you keep talking and talking, they never have an opening to respond. As the band Depeche Mode says, learn to *Enjoy the Silence*.[15] See it as a way to step back and let the other person think about your question, formulate a response, and share. If the other person says they aren't sure or didn't understand the question, don't take it personally. You're learning, and you'll improve with practice. If you get stuck, just ask an empowering question like "where do you want to go from here?"

Some questions can unlock positive emotions and open us up to inspiring possibilities. In their research around coaching for possibility, Richard Boyaztis, Ellen van Oosten, and Melvin Smith from Case Western Reserve University and Angela Passarelli from the College of Charleston and the Institute of Coaching have discovered that certain types of questions can activate "positive emotional attractors" in our brains. That is, asking questions that prompt thinking about possibilities, values, strengths, and our vision for the future can stimulate positive emotions and open new neural pathways. This not only helps us engage in broad, unconstrained, creative thinking, it also facilitates learning and social development, and enables us to feel more open and relaxed.[16]

Research Spotlight: Coaching around possibility

Dr. Angela Passarelli, Associate Professor of Management at the College of Charleston and Director of Research at the Institute of Coaching, on asking big, visionary questions

Us: Angela, what happens when we ask someone a big, visionary, future-focused question?

Dr. Passarelli: When you focus on possibility and not problems in your questions, you give the other person space to be creative, to really think about meaning and purpose, to imagine an ideal future. It also enables human connection.

Us: Amazing that the framing of a question can be so powerful. There is a biological basis for this, right?

Dr. Passarelli: We have done neuroimaging studies that show differences in the brain when you talk about (a) problems versus (b) possibilities. Talking about possibility evokes the PEA (Positive Emotional Attractor) state, which is associated with distinct patterns of activation in the brain. We see activation in brain networks that are associated with big-picture thinking, empathy, openness, and human connection. When we talk about problems, the NEA (Negative Emotional Attractor) is evoked, which involves different networks in the brain – those more associated with narrow thinking (and even a narrower field of vision) and analytical reasoning.

Us: So if I ask you a question about a problem, it literally puts you into this narrow, analytical, problem-solving mindset. But if I ask you a question about what could be possible, it opens you up to creative, unconstrained thinking?

Dr. Passarelli: Correct, although asking about possibility can sometimes be uncomfortable for people at first. If they aren't accustomed to thinking that way, it can trigger a stress response. Imagine being asked for the first time, "Who do you want to be?" or "What do you really want?" It's overwhelming – particularly if what you want is in conflict with messages coming from your organization or society. It can be distressing to say you want something else. But once people break through and identify their true future aspirations, they feel liberated and empowered. It creates a sense of purpose for people that we often lose sight of when we are just going through the day-to-day.

Us: Lots of people focus on solving problems all day long at work. If that's activating the NEA, what are the implications of that for their relationships?

Dr. Passarelli: If you have been working on spreadsheets for two hours and someone pops in to talk to you, you might appear less empathetic or possibly even dehumanize them. The PEA and NEA activate two different, antagonistic networks (the default mode network and test positive networks, respectively). It takes time to switch off analytic mode and switch on empathetic mode. When one network is activated, the other is deactivated. Keep that in mind when your job involves both people management or connecting with people and working in data or problem solving.

Us: How do you want coaches to ask questions differently based on your research?

Dr. Passarelli: I want coaches to stop beginning the coaching conversation with assessment feedback or data. I want them to start the conversation by helping someone explore the ideal future instead. If someone wants to solve an immediate problem, avoid starting with details of the problem and what they have already tried. Instead, start by asking them to articulate the ideal outcome and work backward from that.

If you decide to work on asking more questions, in the early days you might find that you experience pressure or anxiety to come up with *just the right question*. What's ironic about this feeling is that it gets in the way of really listening to what the other person is saying. You get distracted thinking about the next question you want to ask rather than truly listening. One way to relieve some of that pressure is to focus on being curious and noticing. These are two of our favorite skills. Curiosity has magical powers for lifting us out of defensiveness and judgment, and intentional noticing helps us be more mindful and present and focused on what's happening in the moment.

 Experience it yourself

Next time you are having a conversation with someone and you want to practice asking questions, let go of the urge to come up with the perfect question. Instead, practice getting curious. It can be as simple as saying, "I wonder . . . " or "I'm so curious about your trip to the salt cave – tell me more!" or "That experience sounds really unpleasant. I'm curious how you made it through."

When it comes to getting curious and being totally open to how the conversation may unfold, we find that adopting that beginner's mindset, as we mentioned earlier on, can be very helpful. The concept of a beginner's mind comes from Buddhism and suggests that we let go of our preconceived notions and what we believe we already know, so that our minds can be open and free to ideas and possibilities that arise. Letting go of all that you think you already know about a topic, a person, or a situation can open your mind to endless possibilities for where to go with the conversation. Clinging to what you think you already know can introduce bias and narrow your thinking and what you hear in the conversation. For example, let's say you are very experienced at baking bread. Your friend is telling you about their adventures learning how to make sourdough bread. If you do NOT bring a beginner's mind you may find yourself asking narrow and perhaps even judgmental or problem-solving questions ("What temperature was the water when you added it to the yeast?" or "Why didn't you let the oven pre-heat all the way?"). Adopting a beginner's mind and letting go of your preconceived notions will help you be more present with the other person. You can get more curious about their experience, asking questions like "What inspired you to start baking sourdough?" or "How did it taste?" (rather than assuming you know what sourdough tastes like!). In the wise words of Zen Buddhist Shunryu Suzuki,[17] "In the beginner's mind there are many possibilities, but in the expert's mind there are few."

Experience it yourself

Brodie and Shonna make a point of taking on new hobbies or practices on a regular basis to help strengthen their beginner's mindset and encourage their students to do so, too. Choose two new practices – one physical, and one mindfulness practice. They can be anything and don't have to take up much time. To give you some ideas, Shonna once decided to learn how to do the monkey bars. Her practice involved spending 5–10 minutes each day practicing. We've had students start a yoga class or commit to running 20 minutes 3 times each week or use a meditation app every night before bed. The point is to notice what it feels like to go from awkward and effortful to natural and effortless. Consider recording your observations in a journal.

Name it and claim it

Another tool to evoke awareness is what's referred to as direct communication. As you may have noticed in earlier paragraphs, some of the example responses (e.g., "tell me more...") aren't even questions! They are statements that invite the other person to continue, which serves a similar function as asking a question. When you deliberately activate your noticing, curiosity naturally follows, and questions naturally arise when we are curious. Noticing can leverage all our senses – what we see, hear, smell, sense about the other person or situation. The key to noticing is to be objective. If you find yourself judging, thinking "I should do XYZ," jumping to conclusions about things you see or hear, you aren't really noticing. In fact, in their coaching skills workshops for leaders, coaches and facilitators at The Boda Group,[18] an executive coaching firm, encourage not only noticing, but also *naming* what you notice. Noticing and naming can help you stay objective and not move to judgment. For example, if you're having an emotional conversation with your friend, you might notice a very subtle frown and glimmers of tears in the corners of their eyes. Noticing and naming here might open up feelings of care and support for them. To notice and name in this situation, you would simply say, "Friend, I notice that you seem sad" or "you look upset." Keep it simple. You want to be careful to focus on what you are noticing, not labeling the person or jumping to conclusions. For instance, you would say, "You seem sad," not "You are sad." That subtle nuance between "seem" (what I'm noticing) and "are" (my assumptions about what you're experiencing) can keep the person from feeling judged or misunderstood. To truly notice and name, you don't need to dig into why they are feeling that way or try to make them feel better, you simply name what you are noticing about them. Let's try it out.

Experience it yourself

Pause for a moment and look around the space where you are sitting. Notice what you see, hear, or smell. Don't judge or jump to conclusions. You can name things as you notice if it helps (e.g., if you see a stack of papers on your desk, simply say "stack of papers," not "look at that mess!" That's judging!).

_____

_____

_____

As you look around and notice, pick a few things to get curious about (e.g., I'm curious about those big grey clouds I see outside, I'm curious about the new leaves I see sprouting from this houseplant, etc.)

_____

_____

_____

What questions arise for you as you practice your curiosity? (e.g., I wonder if it's going to rain this afternoon? I wonder why that plant seems to grow better in this room than the other room, etc.)

_____

_____

_____

Now, write down a few situations where you think practicing noticing and/or curiosity and questions will help you (or someone else!)

_____

_____

_____

Direct communication

There are many tools for evoking awareness in this category of direct communication. Noticing and naming is one. Another simple but powerful tool is to reflect back a person's own words to them. This is a strategy that is often considered part of *active listening*, where you play back to someone what you just heard. Research has shown that people feel more satisfied with a conversation when their partner or colleague used this active listening strategy of paraphrasing their words back to them. Particularly if someone's thoughts seem a little random, or they are talking in a stream of consciousness, simply paraphrasing back what you heard in one sentence can help them gain clarity and connect the dots between their thoughts. They may respond with, "Yes, that's it!" or, "No, that's not what I meant." Or "Now that I hear you say it back, I see a problem with my line of thinking." An alternative to paraphrasing is using the other person's words directly. This is sometimes referred to as "parroting," but frankly we don't love that term because for some people it has a negative connotation. Here's how it works. Let's say the two of us, Shonna and Brodie, are having a conversation. Brodie says to Shonna, "I am just feeling so overwhelmed. I have this and that and this and that going on." Shonna responds using Brodie's own words, "You feel overwhelmed." Here, Brodie feels seen and heard. She says "YES! I am just so tired of having too much to do all the time," then continues to unpack all the feelings and factors contributing to her sense of overwhelm. In this short example, Shonna is being a great friend and coach – and she hardly said anything at all. The power of playing someone's words back to them is in giving them a chance to hear their own words. It's a way to hold up the mirror for them.

Another way to evoke awareness in others is to offer feedback on what you're hearing and seeing. This is another form of holding up the mirror. If we use the Brodie and Shonna example again, Shonna might say to Brodie, "Brodie this is the third conversation we have had in the last two weeks where you mentioned feeling overwhelmed." In that example, Shonna provided fact-based feedback that held up the mirror to Brodie without judgment or interpretation. Coaching and feedback are natural complements to one another. Asking a coaching question after providing feedback supports the other person is reflecting on their experience. For instance, Shonna could say to Brodie, "This is the third conversation in the last two weeks where you mentioned feeling overwhelmed. What's at the heart of it?" Or, "What would you like to feel instead of overwhelm?" Or, "If you could do anything you wanted, what would you do to get yourself out of this feeling of overwhelm?"

Feedback can be used not only to hold up the mirror, but also to celebrate and encourage progress or successes that you have noticed. Feedback is also powerful for highlighting gaps between what someone says they want and the thoughts and behaviors they're engaging in that are likely to stand in the way of their achievement. Let's go to our Brodie and Shonna example again. Shonna, being a great friend and accountability partner, might share the feedback: "Brodie, when we met last week, you committed to finishing Chapter 4 by Friday. Today is Monday and you are still working on it." Once again, this feedback contains no judgment – it is completely fact-based and Shonna is simply pointing out a gap between what Brodie committed to and her actual behavior.

A key point we want to emphasize here is that your words are a very powerful tool. When it comes to being intentional with language, one of our favorite concepts is *speech acts*, which comes from the book *Language and the Pursuit of Happiness* by Chalmers Brothers.[19] The words that we use speak things into being. We can make declarations, requests, promises, and offers to others. Many of us engage in each of these acts daily without realizing it. When we make a declaration, we assert that we are going to do something, and intentionally or unintentionally we put wheels into motion. For example, when Brodie said, "I will have Chapter 4 finished by Friday," that was a declaration. She was committing to an important milestone that would subsequently drive her behavior. Shonna may have heard that declaration as a *promise* – a commitment to our timeline and our work together. So, when Monday came and Brodie still wasn't finished with Chapter 4, she may have seen it as a missed deadline, but to Shonna it may have been a broken promise ("promise" here can also mean a commitment).

In a coaching conversation, we can be mindful of our own language and raise others' awareness of their language. When we are using our coaching skills, we don't want to give advice. However, we can make an offer. For example, if you are coaching a colleague, you could bring additional perspective into the conversation with "May I offer an observation based on something that I've experienced in the past?" or "May I offer a book recommendation?" It's completely up to the other person whether they accept that offer. Contrast making an offer with "shoulding," such as "You should read this book" or "You should do what I did when I faced a similar situation." Lastly, we can make requests of others based on our ideas, needs, or wants. In the Brodie/Shonna example this could look like Shonna saying, "Brodie I have a request. You can take as much time as you need on Chapter 4. Can you please choose a deadline that is realistic for you so I can anticipate your timing?" Alternatively, Brodie may make a request of Shonna, such as: "Shonna, I have a request. I have hit a wall on Chapter 4. Can I hand it off to you now, even though I didn't finish my section?"

We consider powerful questions and deep listening to be the foundation of your coaching toolkit. These additional tools of naming and direct communication are also impactful ways to evoke awareness in others.

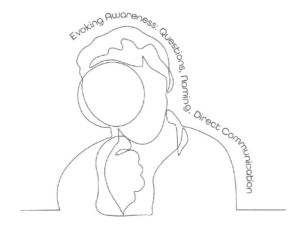

Facilitating growth in others

The fourth coaching competency we mentioned that makes up the core of coaching skills is Facilitating Client Growth. The International Coaching Federation (ICF) defines this competency as "partnering with the client to transform learning and insight into action and promoting client autonomy in the coaching process."[20] This two-pronged definition reinforces some of the points we've tried to make through this book. The first is that coaching is a purposeful conversation. If the conversation ends without a plan for action, it might never lead to the desired change. To ensure the conversation leads to lasting change, coaches help their clients crystalize learnings (e.g., "What was your biggest take away from this conversation?"), incorporate learnings into their worldview (e.g., "How might that shift the way you approach similar situations in the future?"), and invite them to design next steps to further their development and goal pursuit (e.g., "What do you want to do from here? What will get in your way? How will you overcome it?). The second point of "promoting client autonomy" means that the client (or person being coached) is still in the driver's seat. The coach does not assign work or tell the client what to do. The coach asks questions, offers suggestions and encouragement, and partners in accountability. But ultimately the client decides their path forward and what they are willing to commit to. The goal is still to teach the client to fish, not to feed them a fish for a day.

Perhaps you have heard of the GROW coaching model.[21] GROW stands for goals, reality, options, and way forward. This approach to coaching has been widely adopted in organizations as an effective and approachable framework for a coaching conversation. Using this approach, the coaching conversation follows an arc: We start by establishing your goals, both macro (what are you trying to achieve?) and micro (What do you want to get out of this conversation?). You'll notice this is akin to establishing an agreement at the start of the conversation. Once goals have been articulated, the conversation moves on to discussing the current reality. The coach helps the client fully explore their current situation as it pertains to their goal. This segues to the "options" phase where the client gets to have fun coming up with as many potential solutions as possible. Ideally this includes some unconstrained thinking and true exploration of possibility. In the final step, *way forward*, the coach and client pivot to turning insight into action by deciding what path to pursue coming out of the coaching conversation. The client decides which solution they are most excited about (or seems most appropriate) and maps out next steps and commitments. The actual *growth* occurs AFTER the coaching session, when the client follows through on their commitments then stops to reflect on what happened, what worked or did not work, and what they learned from the experience.

Bringing it all together

Let's go back to Casey to consider what the situation might have looked like with a few coaching questions and some direct communication. When Casey got the text from Stella, their mind immediately went to the worst. This is a thought pattern referred to as "awfulizing" and is a very common even if not-so-helpful thing that we humans do. Imagine that you were standing next to Casey in that moment. You might have helped them to avoid the downward spiral by asking them "what else might be going on here?" Imagine you were in a conversation with Casey and they shared the frustration they had with themself about overreacting. You might help them to practice more self-compassion[22] with some direct communication. "It sounds like you're disappointed in yourself for overreacting. What would you say to a friend who had that experience?" You might also use this opportunity to help Casey move beyond the current situation to explore what matters to them. "It sounds like you were pretty triggered by the communication with Stella. What bothered you most about it?" You might have used Casey's responses to help them further explore their beliefs, needs, and values. These tools vary along the continuum we shared from explorative to directive and are all ways to effectively open up new awareness for Casey. Depending on where Casey wants to go with all of this, you could invite planning and offer resources. If Casey wants to focus on stopping the downward cycle of awfulizing, you might ask Casey how they want to respond the next time they feel triggered. You could work with Casey to design some exercises to practice in the next week. You might even offer that they can send you a text message when they feel triggered to help them name it and insert a pause before responding.

In the previous chapters, we reviewed the ways in which our identity, beliefs, values, and emotions impact the data we select and how we interpret them. These same psychological principles apply to everyone you interact with as well. You have a robust set of tools and approaches you have developed throughout your life to engage with others. Coaching skills are not the only answer and they're not necessarily the right tool in every situation. You have been using listening, questions, and direct communication within the context of your relationships your entire life. Focusing on coaching skills and thinking about them as intentional areas of focus you want to further develop are just a way to sharpen them further. Doing so can deepen the level of trust in your relationships.

In Chapter 5, we expand our aperture beyond 1:1 interactions to consider the unique and complex dynamics of groups and teams, and how you can use your coaching mindset and skill set to be more effective in this situations.

Chapter 4 Key idea

Other people have the same challenges and abilities that you have when it comes to emotion, perception, behavior, and cognition. You can use your coaching skills to help draw them out, become aware of the other person's biases and limiting beliefs to have more constructive interactions with them.

Want to learn more? Check out

Learn more about the International Coaching Federation (ICF) coaching competencies by visiting their website, coachingfederation.org, where you can also access videos about each competency.

To invest in developing your listening skills, check out "How to Become a Better Listener" by Robin Abrahams and Boris Groysberg, published in *Harvard Business Review* in December 2021.

Recommended reading

The advice trap by Michael Bungay-Stanier

Change your questions, change your life by Marilee Adams

Feedback fundamentals and evidence-based best practices by Brodie Gregory Riordan

The surprising science of meetings by Steve Rogelberg

You're not listening by Kate Murphy

Notes

1 Wildman, J. L., Bedwell, W. L., Salas, E., & Smith-Jentsch, K. A. (2011). Performance measurement at work: A multilevel perspective. In *APA handbook of industrial and organizational psychology: Building and developing the organization* (Vol. 1). American Psychological Association. https://doi.org/10.1037/12169-010

2 International Coaching Federation. (2021). *ICF core competencies.* https://coachfederation.org/core-competencies

3 Dweck, C. (2016, January 13). What having a "growth mindset" actually means. *Harvard Business Review.* https://hbr.org/2016/01/what-having-a-growth-mindset-actually-means

4 Passmore, J., & Sinclair, T. (2020). Foundation domain, competency 2: Embodies a coaching mindset. In *Becoming a coach: The essential ICF guide* (pp. 57–63). Springer. https://doi.org/10.1007/978-3-030-53161-4_7

5 International Coaching Federation. (2020). *ICF global coaching study.* https://coachfederation.org/app/uploads/2020/09/FINAL_ICF_GCS2020_Executive Summary.pdf

6 www.coachingfederation.org

7 Rogelberg, S. G. (2018). *The surprising science of meetings: How you can lead your team to peak performance.* New York: Oxford University Press.

8 Whitworth, L., Kimsey-House, K., Kimsey-House, H., & Sandhal, P. (2009). *Co-Active coaching.* Boston, MA: Davies-Black.

9 Itzchakov, G., & Kluger A. N. (2018, May 17). The power of listening in helping people change. *Harvard Business Review.* https://hbr.org/2018/05/the-power-of-listening-in-helping-people-change

10 Huang, K., Yeomans, M., Brooks, A. W., Minson, J., & Gino, F. (2017). It doesn't hurt to ask: Question-asking increases liking. *Journal of Personality and Social Psychology, 113*(3), 430–452. https://doi.org/10.1037/pspi0000097

11 Gregory, J. B., & Levy, P. E. (2010). Employee coaching relationships: Enhancing construct clarity and measurement. *Coaching: An International Journal of Theory, Research and Practice, 3*(2), 109–123. https://doi.org/10.1080/17521882.2010.502901

Gyllensten, K., & Palmer, S. (2007). The coaching relationship: An interpretive phenomenological analysis. *International Coaching Psychology Review, 2*(2), 168–177.

12 Brooks, A. W., & John, L. K. (2018, May–June). The surprising power of questions. *Harvard Business Review.* https://hbr.org/2018/05/the-surprising-power-of-questions

13 Bungay-Stanier, M. (2020). *The advice trap: Be humble, stay curious & change the way you lead forever.* Toronto, ON CA: Box of Crayons Press.

14 Waters, S. D., & Kraiger, K. (In press). Training and learning strategies. In R. Silzer, B. R Scott & W. C. Borman. (Eds.), *Handbook on the practice of industrial/organizational psychology: Leveraging psychology for individual and organizational effectiveness.* Oxford University Press.

15 Gore, M. (1989). Enjoy the Silence [Recorded by Depeche Mode]. *Violator.* Mute Records.

16 Boyatzis, R. E., Smith, M., & Van, O. E. (2019). *Helping people change: Coaching with compassion for lifelong learning and growth.* Boston: Harvard Business Press.

17 www.shambhala.com/zen-mind-beginner-s-mind-1796.html

18 https://bodagroup.com/

19 Brothers, C. (2005). *Language and the pursuit of happiness.* Naples, FL: New Possibilities Press.

20 ICF. (2021). *Competencies.*

21 Downey, M. (1999). *Effective coaching.* London: Orion Business Books.

22 Neff, K., & Knox, M. C. (2016). Self-compassion. In *Mindfulness in positive psychology: The science of meditation and wellbeing* (Vol. 37, pp. 1–8). New York: Routledge.

5
Using a coaching approach in groups and teams

Questions we'll answer in this chapter:

1. How do the concepts we've discussed so far impact group dynamics?
2. How can a coaching mindset make you a more effective teammate?
3. How can coaching skills be used with groups and teams?

Jin was exhausted. He was recently promoted into a leadership role in the sales organization. Although he had a sales role early in his career, he had been working in Operations when the role became available. He had built strong relationships with his senior leaders and was thrilled when he was offered the role. Taking on the team was another matter. After his promotion was announced, he had an all-hands meeting to set the tone. He carefully crafted a presentation where he shared his background and qualifications and his vision for the department, including where he saw opportunities for improvement. As he settled into his new role, he quickly noticed tension with the team. When issues arose, he often disagreed with how the team was responding. Feedback started pouring in about missteps the team had made or customers who were upset. Jin felt even more under pressure to get things back on track – quickly.

Mateo, one of the long-tenured leaders reporting to Jin, shared with Jin during a one-on-one that the team wasn't feeling supported. They didn't think that Jin was on their side. At first, Jin was angry. He didn't feel like he could be on their side when they were making mistakes. His job was to improve the performance of the department, and they weren't behind him. That certainly wasn't helping *him*, and it wasn't doing the team any favors either. Jin knew that he couldn't be successful unless he could get things back on track with his team. He wasn't sure how to fix it. He felt stuck. The team didn't trust him and he didn't trust the team. He considered just

DOI: 10.4324/9781003166917-7

replacing everyone, but if he did that, it basically guaranteed that they'd miss their revenue numbers for at least two quarters, and he'd be starting from scratch with a new team.

In Chapter 4, we described the ways in which a coaching mindset and skill set can be used to improve relationships between two people. We talked about these interactions as a collision between two icebergs. As our interactions expand from one-on-one to groups of people, we find ourselves navigating a sea of icebergs. Sailing might be faster and smoother without all those icebergs in the way, but most of us don't live or work in a calm, quiet, pristine sea on our own. To accomplish big things, we need all those icebergs (aka people) to come together. In his *Harvard Business Review* interview with Diane Coutu, seasoned teams expert and professor of social and organizational psychology at Harvard University Richard Hackman notes that in team settings the benefits of collaboration and multiple perspectives are often overshadowed by the hassles of coordination and challenges to individual motivation.[1]

As we mentioned in Chapter 1, humans evolved as social creatures. In fact, our survival was dependent on being part of a group.[2] We were no match physically for our environmental predators, so we learned to depend on others. People developed cognitive skills to build tools to overcome our physical limitations and social skills to lean on each other for physical protection, social connection, and to solve complex problems. This dependence on social groups resulted in a primal need for inclusion. Exclusion or rejection from the group could result in death. This meant that the leader of the group bore a great deal of responsibility for the safety of the group members and therefore held a great deal of power.

We might not be working together to outsmart lions anymore, but these characteristics are still present in modern groups and teams. A group is two or more individuals who do not necessarily share common goals or have interdependent tasks. An example of a group might be high potentials in an organization, a running group, or a book club. Groups may share characteristics and goals, but their success is not interdependent. Your growth and success as a high-potential leader in an organization may be unrelated to the growth and success of your peers. You can finish reading the book club book even if your book club friends don't (although the discussion might not be as rich!). In contrast, a team is two or more individuals who share common goals and have interdependent tasks. If the group of high potentials is given a project to do together and each member's part is dependent on the work of the others, they become a team. On a running team, every member's score contributes to a team score. As the world of work evolves, it continues to get more complex and interdependent. In fact, in contemporary organizations, learning and innovation primarily occur at the team level.[3]

The power and perils of teams

Group and team settings introduce a dynamic mix of beliefs, emotions, and behaviors that can create the need for and the opportunity to catalyze energy and behavior change. It could be that you want to influence what book the group reads next. Maybe you think your team at work needs to change course to achieve a goal or target. One way of influencing this direction is to assert yourself – even take a "my way or the highway" approach. That will probably work in the short-term for getting people to do what you want. But they would probably be more excited about the book and likely to get the reading done each month if they had a say or felt a personal attachment to the solution, too.

It's one thing to identify and align your own thinking and actions to a goal, but getting others on board is a different challenge. This complexity also comes with advantages. People look for social connection, belonging, social learning or modeling, and shared accountability, which can all be facilitated in a group setting. In other words, shifting from individual or dyadic relationships to groups and teams creates the opportunity to solve bigger and more complex challenges – not just because you have more brains and brawn to apply to it, but because being affiliated with a group taps into another level of motivation.

Decades of psychological research have demonstrated the link between basic human needs and motivation:[4]

- Community (or relatedness) – the need for belonging and attachment to others
- Autonomy – the need to feel in control of our own destiny (i.e., our behaviors and goals)
- Mastery (or competence) – the need to master tasks and learn new skills; people want to be good at the work they do
- Purpose – the need to contribute something bigger than themselves

When needs are met in a work context, employees can think more creatively. They are more open to diverse perspectives that fuel innovation; more open and empathetic to working with others and are more engaged and productive. Research shows that highly engaged employees innovate more and think more creatively than disengaged employees, persevere through challenges, create 10% better customer experiences, are 20% more productive, are 59% less likely to quit, and drive higher profits.

When individuals feel psychologically safe and as though their core needs are being met, they are more likely to collaborate effectively with and be open to the perspectives of others. This is important, as most workplaces have been on an upward trajectory of greater and greater collaboration. For instance, research from Corporate Executive Board[5] (CEB, now Gartner) found that there has been a 50% increase in the number of individuals involved in making decisions, and 67% of respondents reported an increase in the amount of work that requires collaboration with others. These workplace changes can provide new opportunities for a sense of community, and they can also make work feel harder, more complex, slower, and less autonomous. Rob Cross, a professor at Babson University, noticed the stressful demands of more and more collaboration, particularly on high performers in organizations. His observations prompted him to identify the concept of *collaborative overload*, which occurs when individuals – typically high performers – are overwhelmed with collaborative demands (such as requests from colleagues, meetings, collaborative projects, etc.) to the extent that they struggle to have time for their own work. Like the research from CEB, Rob Cross and colleagues found that collaborative work for some has increased by 50% over the last two decades.[6] They discovered that, in many organizations, people spend up to 80% of their time in meetings, on calls, or responding to emails and requests. 80%!! As a result, their individual work tasks often get pushed to evenings and weekends, leading to fatigue, burnout, and increased feelings of stress.

Time demands aside, simply working with and navigating a wide variety of personalities and perspectives throughout the day is challenging and demanding. It requires listening, attention, adaptability, and self-regulation – all of which utilize our cognitive resources. We propose that your coaching skills and coaching mindset can help you more effectively navigate these complex interpersonal dynamics and increased demands for collaboration. Before we get into that, let's pause to connect this to one of your experiences.

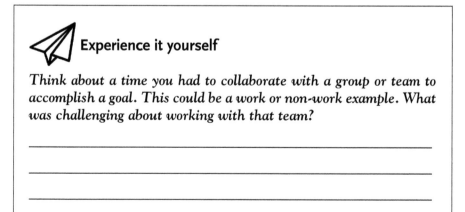

Experience it yourself

Think about a time you had to collaborate with a group or team to accomplish a goal. This could be a work or non-work example. What was challenging about working with that team?

_____

_____

_____

What worked well with the team?

_____

_____

_____

In what way was the team able to accomplish more than an individual working alone?

_____

_____

_____

How did your own level of satisfaction and engagement influence your openness and collaboration with the team?

_____

_____

_____

Looking back on that experience, what would YOU do the same or differently if you were to work with that team again?

_____

_____

_____

Leader as coach

Coaching skills can be used to tap into the motivational potential of groups and teams. Using the core coaching skills of listening deeply (and listening to understand) and asking questions to draw out ideas and raise awareness can surface and begin to address common team dysfunctions. In Chapter 2 we explored the biases and assumptions that influence our thinking and behavior every day. In group and team settings, those biases and assumptions influence the way we interpret others' behaviors and how we choose to behave. In his book *The Five Dysfunctions of a Team*,[7] Patrick Lencioni notes that a lack of trust among team members can adversely affect their performance.

Running up the ladder of inference in interpreting a team member's words or actions will stifle not only our willingness to trust them, but also the likelihood that we will be vulnerable and gain their trust.

Let's take Jin from our story at the start of the chapter. Jin doesn't trust his team, and they don't trust him. Jin is new to leading this team, and his impressions have been influenced by chatter about the team's ineffectiveness. From the very start, Jim assumes the team is low performing. His preference is to replace them all, if only that wouldn't be disruptive in the short term. Imagine how Jin's assumptions about the team influence the way he engages with them. If we could capture a day in the life of Jin and his team, we would see that he spends most of the day alone in his office with the door closed, trying to put out fires himself and figure out how to right the ship that he has inherited. Jin's team is composed of leaders of various tenures, who have worked together for several years and generally have good working dynamics. The team sees Jin's isolated behavior and assumes he is uninterested in getting to know them and understanding the scope and challenges of their work. Members of the team roll their eyes to each other when Jin sends communications to the team and gossip over coffee about what they think will happen to his role.

In short, both Jin and the leaders on his team are failing to build trust or seek to understand. By making assumptions and avoiding direct communication, the disconnect between the team and their new leader grows wider each day. What would happen if – instead of holing up in his office most of the day – Jin set up coffee chats with each team member and sincerely sought to understand their role, their challenges, and get to know them as a person? By sharing his own doubts and challenges so far in the role, Jin would show vulnerability that would open the door for team members to understand and trust him more. Instead of gossiping over coffee and rolling their eyes at his emails, what if his team members led with curious questions? So often the challenges and disconnects within a team stem from these very behaviors: making assumptions, avoiding a conversation that feels scary (in fact, another of Patrick Lencioni's five dysfunctions of a team is *avoiding conflict!*), practicing judgment rather than curiosity, and not seeking to understand.

By practicing their coaching skills leaders can shape team culture and create psychological safety and an environment where people feel empowered and safe to innovate and take risks and work in agile ways. In a recent *Harvard Business Review* article, researchers explain that 70% of managers consider themselves "inspirational" figures who create purpose, passion, and intrinsic motivation for their teams. Yet, 82% of surveyed employees *don't* see their managers this way.[8] That's a major disconnect! This gap indicates two things. First, managers often lack self-awareness about the degree to which they are embodying the role of inspirational leader. Second, managers generally *want* to be inspirational and create the conditions that create high performance teams. Learning and practicing inspirational leadership behaviors drives the performance outcomes organizations seek. The extent to which a leader practices inspirational behaviors predicts levels of trust among team members, team member commitment to the team, and, in turn, team performance. This connection between inspirational leadership and outcomes is even higher when the team is dispersed geographically.

In Chapter 2, we discussed the role of emotions. We know that emotions can impact your own behavior and the behavior of others. There's also scientific evidence that emotions can spread to others and influence the collective emotion of the group.[9] This is known as emotional contagion.[10] The collective effect of contagion has an impact on outcomes such as collaboration. Any group member can impact the broader group or team through these processes. Leaders, however, have an outsized impact. Research from BetterUp[11] found that leaders low in resilience have 23% lower performing teams. When leaders have low mental agility, their teams are 29% less agile, and when they lack strategic thinking skills, team innovation drops by 23%. When leaders lack skills like emotional regulation, turnover intentions of their direct reports rise by 13%. Leaders who invest the time and effort to become self-aware, develop their emotion regulation skills, cultivate their own resilience, and learn key coaching tools and strategies (like noticing, naming, reframing) are the ones who bring out the best in their teams and create conditions for success.

Team member as coach

These mindsets and behaviors are not just relevant for leaders. Individual team members also influence the experience of their teammates and the efficacy of the team as a whole. Research has shown that teams with high self-awareness (that is, individual team members have high self-awareness and therefore the team has high collective self-awareness) are both higher functioning and higher performing.[12] Emotional contagion within teams can create a shared sense of affect or emotion within a team. Research by Totterdell and colleagues showed that certain characteristics of individual team members determine how much their mood will be influenced by the collective team mood. In their study with teams of nurses, these researchers found that nurses who were older, seen as more committed to their team, and had more positive perceptions of the team culture were more likely to "catch" the collective mood of the team. In another study, Totterdell found that cricket players perceived their own level of performance as higher when they played on teams that had higher levels of shared happiness.[13] And, teams that experience positive emotional contagion – which can start with a single team member – have higher levels of cooperation and lower levels of group conflict.[14]

While group cohesion can be important for trust and performance, having the courage to speak up or share a dissenting view can also enhance the performance of the team. In his work, Harvard's Richard Hackman found that high-performing teams must have at least one "deviant"[15] who can raise tough questions and challenge norms and expectations. To demonstrate, let's revisit Mateo, one of Jin's direct reports. Mateo demonstrates caring and courage by sharing with Jin that the team feels unsupported. But Mateo's real impact on the situation begins when he decides to engage differently with his teammates in their discussions about Jin. When one long-time teammate, Carol, opens a Zoom call with three other teammates by making a disparaging joke about Jin's leadership, Mateo – rather than laughing awkwardly like the others – uses a speech act (remember those from Chapter 4?) of *declaring* and states, "I want to find a way to help Jin succeed in his role." Silence follows, then another teammate chimes in, "Mateo, I agree. I don't want to have a revolving door of leaders. I would like to see Jin succeed, too." By making this one simple statement, Mateo has opened up a new path forward for the team's relationship with Jin. Mateo took a big risk by speaking up. Teams who have at least one outspoken member who is willing to dissent tend to be significantly more innovative, and less prone to groupthink. However, the individual who speaks up often risks personal social capital;[16] team members who are put off by their questions or who favor consensus may retaliate or box out the dissenting team member. When team members adopt their CON (curious, open, non-judgmental) mindset, they will be more willing to hear others' perspectives, including those of dissent.

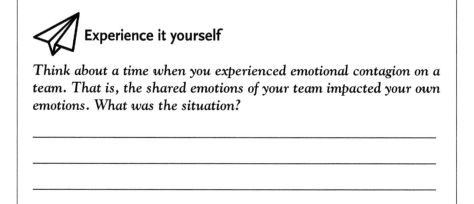

Experience it yourself

Think about a time when you experienced emotional contagion on a team. That is, the shared emotions of your team impacted your own emotions. What was the situation?

_____

_____

_____

What impact did those emotions have on you? In other words, how did positive emotions enhance your experience? How did negative emotions adversely affect your experience?

_____

_____

_____

Who was most influential in contributing to the shared emotions of the team? What was their impact?

_____

_____

_____

How did you self-manage through that experience?

_____

_____

_____

 Experience it yourself

Intention challenge! Set an intention to have every person who you interact with tomorrow leave the interaction feeling more positive and optimistic than they were before you interacted with them. Journal about what you notice from this experiment.

Shifting roles

One person's role on a team can morph and evolve with time and changing demands or goals. And one person may play many very different roles across different teams. Let's take Brodie, for example. At one point in her career, Brodie was an individual contributor on a team at work. Within a few years, she was co-leading that team with a peer and had several direct reports, some of whom had previously been peers. Her role on that team evolved over time, and therefore so did her relationships. At the same time, Brodie was on a cross-functional project team in the organization with an entirely different group of people. Within her local office, she was a member of a team that co-ordinated community service projects. This team comprised people she never worked with in her role, from completely different parts of the business. She also led an affinity group focused on programming and events for women in the office – another role that was separate from her core work team. Outside of work, Brodie led a team of coaches doing pro-bono work for a non-profit. She was a member of a weekly running group and of a non-profit board, which she eventually went on to lead. From this example alone, Brodie was a member of six very distinct teams. The dynamics of each team were vastly different, and so was the role that Brodie filled on each team. On two of those teams her role shifted and evolved as membership changed and she became more tenured.

In addition to the fluid nature of one's role on a team at any given time, the way they *perceive* their role on the team can be equally important. Think back to Chapter 1, where we met Marie. Marie's lens on her role in a team is that she pulls more weight than all her teammates, that she works harder than they do, that she is smarter and more competent than they are. She sees her role on her core team as being the "informal leader." Though her boss is *actually* the leader, Marie sees herself as the one who really knows what's going on and who has the best ability to tell other teammates what to do. How do you think Marie's teammates see her role? Quite possibly they see her as an equal who thinks she is superior. Her need to be "on" 24 hours a day often results in her acting like a martyr to the rest of the team, who prefer to be finished with work for the day when they log off. Marie's low self-aware-ness and inaccurate perceptions of her role on the team often create touchy dynamics with her teammates and unnecessary clarification conversations.

Remember that we create our reality through our own lens of perception. When teammates all perceive and experience the same situation a little differently, team cohesion and performance can suffer. It's easy to attribute problems and team dysfunction to "them" – which often translates to a vague sense of everyone else. We are the hero in our own story and as a result often struggle to notice our own contributions to challenging dynamics or clunky collaboration. In her *Harvard Business Review* article, author Jennifer Porter notes that leaders and team members often lack both "internal" and "ex-ternal" self-awareness, which clouds their ability to see the impact they are having in team dysfunction.[17] She notes that internal self-awareness pertains to our ability to be in touch with and aware of our "inner narrative" – our values, thoughts, and beliefs – whereas external self-awareness pertains to our ability to understand the impact of our words and actions on others. These blind spots can prevent us from seeing our own role and thus hold us back from changing our behavior.

In Chapter 2 we discussed the mental shortcuts (biases, heuristics, stereotypes) that influence our thinking and the way that we perceive the world. These same shortcuts and ego-protection mechanisms often distort our perceptions of ourselves and ability to be self-aware. Our tools of pausing, noticing, and reflecting can help us create the mental space to notice how we are showing up and impacting the team. Intentional reflection has been shown to increase self-awareness in a wide array of contexts – from leadership development programs[18] to sports[19] to recovery from trauma.[20] The reflection/self-awareness link also leads to more effective self-monitoring and self-regulation – that is, observing and monitoring our behavior and intentionally regulating or choosing our behavior. In team settings, pausing to notice and reflect on our behavior, therefore, can help us become more self-aware and intentionally choose behaviors that enable us to be better teammates and contributors to the team.

Let's go back to our example of Jin and his team. A few pages ago you also met Carol, another of Jin's direct reports. She was the one making disparaging remarks about Jin's leadership on the team Zoom call. Later that day Carol was out for a bike ride. She couldn't stop ruminating on Mateo's comments about wanting Jin to succeed as their leader. When Mateo spoke up in the moment, Carol felt ashamed and uncomfortable. She felt her face turn pink and got very quiet. On her bike ride, Carol asks herself questions: "Why did I make that comment about Jin?" "How did I get so jaded about our team?" "Is this really how I want to show up at work?" Carol feels like she's letting her mind wander, but really, she is engaging in self-reflection about her behavior that day. She has a sudden realization that she has turned into "that coworker" who is snarky and negative, and who relishes in the failure of others. As she crests a hill on her bike and stops to look at the sunset, she *declares* to herself that she is going to show up differently tomorrow. Mateo was right. She wants to give Jin the benefit of the doubt, too, and start doing things that help and support him, rather than criticize, doubt, and undermine him.

In the example above, Carol used self-reflection to become more self-aware. She didn't like what she discovered, so she intentionally chose to behave differently at work the next day. How can you use this approach in your own team experiences?

Experience it yourself

Think of a team that you are a part of (work, personal, sports, volunteering, etc.). It can be the same team you reflected on earlier or a different one. What role are you playing on that team (not just your formal role, but how do you "show up" or behave on the team)?

_____

_____

_____

What impact does your behavior have on the team as a whole and individual team members?

_____

_____

_____

What role would you like to be playing on that team? How do you want to "show up?"

_____

_____

_____

What behaviors do you need to start doing or stop doing in order to create that role for yourself?

_____

_____

_____

Up, down, all around

Your coaching skills of listening, noticing, and asking great questions will support you in being a more productive and constructive team member in nearly any situation. We find that many people assume coaching skills are only appropriate to use with direct reports or people who are junior to them. We believe that, regardless of your position or role, you can leverage your coaching skills in all directions to have more effective interactions and bring out the best in others. It might feel weird to try to initiate a coaching conversation with your boss or a senior leader, which is one reason why we emphasize coaching *skills* here, as opposed to an across-the-board coaching approach. In other words, you can use your listening skills – a key part of coaching – in any kind of conversation. Asking curious, open-ended questions will also serve you well in any conversation, not just a coaching conversation. Your coaching mindset of being curious, open, and non-judgmental (CON) will enable you to be open to possibility and seeking to understand in your conversations with teammates, peers, bosses, frenemies, and more. It will invite the people you interact with to engage in exploration for themselves and with others and create more possibilities. By practicing your curiosity, openness, and being non-judgmental, you can be a whole new kind of CON artist.

A new kind of CON artist

Recently, our friend, Myra, shared an observation with us about levels of listening on her team at work. She noticed that one member of her team, Trevor, only ever seemed to listen at level 1. No matter who was talking or what they were talking about, he always responded with something about himself. At first Myra found it fascinating and a little amusing – he was truly skilled at finding ways to relate anything and everything to himself!

But then she started to worry about the impact his behavior was having on feelings of inclusion within the team. She noticed that one team member, Chastity, seemed to shut down and stop sharing anytime Trevor responded about himself. Myra debated what to do – should I give him feedback? Share what I'm noticing? Although she felt like that was the right thing to do, Myra simply didn't have the emotional energy for that conversation. Instead, she decided to experiment with her own behavior in those team settings. Anytime Trevor would listen at level 1 and respond about himself, Myra immediately jumped back in and picked up the thread with the other colleague. Here's a snippet from one team meeting about planning for an upcoming retreat:

Chastity: *Okay team, now that we have a clear agenda for the retreat, let's talk about the fun stuff. We have all of Tuesday afternoon and evening set aside for team building and team fun. Last week I asked everyone to submit ideas for what you would like to do, and it looks like the clear frontrunner is the "pints and paints" class that the local art studio hosts at the brewery downtown.*

Trevor: *Yeah, I am not into that. I suggested that we go to a baseball game. What could be more fun than that? It's the perfect time of year to be outside, we can all talk and hang out, it can be dinner, happy hour, and an activity all in one. I already reached out to group sales to get information on tickets for the team. I have lined up a pretty good deal for us, and it also includes a $40 food credit for each of us.*

Myra: *Chastity – thank you for polling the team ahead of time to come up with ideas. Tell us more about the "pints and paints" option.*

In this simple example, Myra used her skills of listening and noticing to ensure Chastity didn't feel shut down or dismissed by Trevor's level 1 listening. Myra brought the conversation back to the original focus and invited Chastity to share more information about the idea that the team had voted on. Now, context is important in this example. If Trevor was a team member who rarely spoke up or shared a perspective, the team might have been more interested in what he had to say. But his pattern of listening at level 1 and making everything about him has gotten very tiresome to the team. If either Myra or Chastity were feeling especially patient and generous, later they might ask Trevor to share more about his baseball idea to seek to understand his intentions. Would that really be an effective team outing, or is it simply something Trevor wants to do on the company's dime?

> ### ✈ Experience it yourself
>
> *What is one team or group setting where adopting a mindset of being curious, open, and non-judgmental (CON) will benefit you and the group or team? How so?*
>
> _____
>
> _____
>
> _____
>
> *How will you leverage your coaching skills of noticing, listening, and asking questions to be a more effective teammate and bring out the best in your team/teammates?*
>
> _____
>
> _____
>
> _____

Using your skill set with intention

Earlier we mentioned the many varied roles that Brodie plays on different teams. The ways that these roles shifted over time highlight the importance of flexibility in how we think about ourselves and our ability to use the various tools in our toolkit with agility and intention. In this book, we've focused on coaching as a powerful tool that you can add to your toolbox regardless of your role. And it's not the only tool in the box. Within a given role, relationship, or even conversation, you might find that using a more directive approach is more helpful than a non-directive approach like coaching. Even within the coaching context, a coach may wear different "hats" as appropriate to meet the team member's needs. To that end, we like to think of organizations as providing a developmental ecosystem. As we mentioned in Chapter 4, each role you play or tool you leverage can be the right one if it is in service to the needs of the situation or person. This means that it's often unnecessary to think of which "hat" to wear, but rather *when* each hat is most useful.

Source: BetterUp

Let's return to Jin and Mateo's situation and see how this range of approaches can be applied. Mateo doesn't feel supported by his manager, Jin. Mateo decides to talk to his previous boss, Sharmane, about it. Sharmane practices focused (level 2) listening as Mateo describes the situation and what he has been experiencing. As she pauses, she considers how to respond. She has been a manager for a long time and has a few decades of her own experiences she could draw from. She could be directive and give Mateo advice on how to have a conversation with Jin about it or how to navigate expressing his concerns to HR. She might offer some evidence-based tools and suggestions on how he can engage with Jin to strengthen their relationship. She could put on her mentor hat and offer ways he can seek out the support he needs from other sources or share stories from similar experiences she had and how she navigated them. Sharmane could also choose to simply ask questions to help Mateo explore what the real issue is and what's most difficult about the situation for him. Sharmane sees each of these paths as potentially helpful to Mateo and appropriate given the content and nature of their relationship. She decides to *ask* Mateo what would be most helpful to him in the moment. Mateo responds that what would be most helpful is to hear Sharmane's advice. He always really valued her input when they worked together, and he's feeling stuck, emotionally drained; he is just searching for ideas. Sharmane decides to honor his request and gives him some advice, including giving him options about how he could consider escalating his concerns to leadership. She acknowledges that she doesn't have the full context and that Mateo is the expert on the situation. He thanks her for the advice but says he's not ready to escalate. Sharmane sees this as an opening and shifts into her more explorative tools. "Mateo, I noticed you winced a bit when I mentioned escalation. How do you want to approach this?" Mateo realizes that he wants to be part of the solution. He wants to give Jin a chance to change and wants to give it his all to help shift the trajectory. "How will you feel if it doesn't work out?" Sharmane asks. Mateo pauses. "I'll feel at peace. I'll know I did the best I could to support Jin and try to make it work. If it doesn't, then I can make a conscious decision to make a change for myself or to share my perspective with someone outside of the team. But it's only fair to Jin to give him a chance to respond to feedback first." "I noticed your jaw relax and your shoulders drop when you said that," Sharmane shared with a smile. "Yes," Mateo said, "that feels good."

Impact on diversity and inclusion

We've talked about basic human needs that evolved through an evolutionary bias for survival. Affiliation, acceptance, and belonging in a group are necessary preconditions to unlock potential, because they are core to our feelings of security. Only 31% of employees agree that their leaders promote an inclusive team environment[21] and underrepresented group members are 1.6 times more likely to have low feelings of belonging.[22] We have seen the impact of a coaching mindset and coaching skills in positively impacting this situation. Humility, curiosity, and empathy are required to fully see, hear, and honor diverse perspectives. These skills are required to explore our own individual relationships with diversity, equity, inclusion, and belonging and in our relationships with others. Coaching conversations can support inclusion and belonging by helping others explore the mindsets and beliefs underlying their experience. In her work on inclusion and belonging on coaching, Salma Shah notes that leaders, managers, and coaches can use their coaching skills to cultivate trust and help create a sense of psychological safety for others.[23] Using your coaching skills of really listening, being fully present for the other person, showing empathy, bringing your CON (curious, open, non-judgmental) mindset, and asking questions can create space for individuals of all backgrounds and identities to feel seen and heard. Take the scenario below, about Felicia's experience.

Felicia: *I had recently joined a new team at work. Three other female colleagues invited me to lunch with them, which was nice. I was excited to get to know them better. Once we were settled in the office cafeteria, the three of them just started complaining about their partners, all of whom were men. It definitely wasn't what I was expecting to happen at lunch but figured maybe they just needed to talk about it. Then one of them turned to me abruptly and said, "Felicia, what about your husband? What does he do for a living?" I paused for a moment and tried to figure out how to respond. I felt a little hijacked – I guess they had no way of knowing that I'm a lesbian and the sole income generator for our family, since my partner takes care of our three kids and two dogs. I felt uncomfortable and didn't want to share because I assumed they would judge me and my wife, based on their assumption that I was married to a man who works full time, and because of the way they were talking about their spouses. At that moment I remember thinking "What am I doing here?"*

In Felicia's example, her colleagues' behavior felt uncomfortable, but most of all their assumptions and leading questions about Felicia's life felt not inclusive. As you know from earlier chapters of this book, we all see life through our own lens of perception, and our beliefs and assumptions are colored by our own experiences, priorities, and values. In Felicia's case, her colleagues assumed that her life was just like their own: That she was married to a man who also worked full time. Despite their behavior, Felicia's colleagues may have had good intentions of getting to know her, but their approach came across as narrow and not inclusive. Instead, they could have asked a more open-ended and curious question, like "Felicia, tell us about your family" or "Felicia, what is life like for you outside of work?" or even "Felicia, how was your weekend?" In Chapter 4 we discussed the value of having a "beginner's mind" and starting from a place of not knowing and not making assumptions. Bringing a beginner's mindset to our interactions with others can help us stay open to all the possibilities of their lives, personality, and experiences and create a more inclusive experience.

But that's not Felicia's only experience with colleague behavior that wasn't inclusive.

Felicia: *After lunch, I got back to my desk, sat down, and let out a big sigh. Another new teammate, who sits across from me, asked what was wrong. I know her intentions were good, but what she did next only made me feel even less like I belonged on this team. I shared about the experience I had just had at lunch and said that I felt uncomfortable and like I didn't fit in with them. She responded by saying that I "shouldn't feel that way and shouldn't let them get to me." Again, I know she had good intentions, but it felt dismissive – like the way I felt didn't really matter. I didn't feel seen, I didn't feel heard. It doesn't feel supportive or inclusive to be told that you shouldn't feel something that you feel.*

Felicia's colleague (let's call her Amber) was trying to show caring and concern for her. But she favored her own discomfort with the topic over truly listening to and being present with Felicia.

⊿ **Experience it yourself**

If Felicia was new to your team and you went to lunch together, what would you have asked her instead?

_____

_____

_____

If you were Felicia's colleague, Amber, what would you have done or said when she shared about her experience at lunch?

_____

_____

_____

If Felicia's colleague, Amber, had a robust set of coaching skills, there are many ways she could have more constructively engaged in this moment. If she practiced really listening, she would have picked up on the emotion that Felicia was expressing. She then could have named what she picked up on, such as "Felicia you sound weary from that conversation" or simply affirmed: "That sounds like an uncomfortable conversation." Noticing and affirming are such simple ways to help another person feel seen and heard, which is likely to make them feel a greater sense of inclusion and belonging. Amber also could have asked a question, such as, "How are you feeling now?" or "What can I do to support you?" or "Tell me more about your experience at lunch." By adopting her CON (curious, open, non-judgmental) mindset, Amber could have created the space and safety for Felicia to open up about her experience and feel a greater sense of inclusion with at least one member of her new team. Although feelings of inclusion and belonging often pertain to a group, team, or even culture fit, ultimately the everyday actions of individuals contribute to or erode those feelings. Bringing your coaching mindset and skills to each interaction can help you to create a more positive experience for those around you.

Group coaching

So far in this chapter we have focused on using a coaching skill set and mindset to be a more effective leader and teammate and have better communication and interactions with the team. In addition to the practice of coaching skills with our colleagues, two formal coaching solutions are also relevant in the group and team context: Group coaching and team coaching.

Group coaching has roots in both organizational development (OD) and group therapy. The OD tradition incorporates process interventions that assist the group in becoming aware of how they operate and how they work together, and how to use this knowledge to solve their own problems. Group coaching targets individual behavior change and focuses on individual challenges and opportunities but unfolds in a group setting. Participants in the group are not necessarily part of an intact team outside the context of the coaching session. Evidence of the effectiveness of group coaching is still building, but a meta-analysis of cognitive-behavioral therapy (CBT) in group therapeutic context suggests that there is potential for positive outcomes.[24] Research has shown that individuals make greater progress on their goals in individual coaching than in group coaching,[25] but group coaching has other advantages, including social support and lower cost. In fact, research on group therapy has shown that social support is not just "nice to have," it can lead to individuals reaching greater progress toward their goals and desired outcomes.[26]

Practice Spotlight

Dr. Alison O'Malley, Director of People Insights & Transformation, Mix Talent Consulting, on group coaching

Us: Ali, you offer group coaching in your work. What is group coaching?

Dr. O'Malley: In my approach to group coaching, small groups of roughly 5 to 8 employees come together on a regular cadence to explore a topic (e.g., feedback) or set of topics. Although there is a lightly held agenda for the arc of the experience and everyone comes in having prepared or practiced with the same learning resources or exercises, the group members shape where each session goes based on what is most important to them.

Us: How did the need or idea for group coaching arise in your organization?

Dr. O'Malley: We wanted to experiment with a more scalable way to embed coaching in our rapidly growing organization. Adopting group coaching allowed us to ensure all people leaders could receive coaching at once. A large number of employees joined during the pandemic – we had people who have been here a year and have never met a coworker in person – and the social bonds fostered through being in the same group are often very strong. Thus, group coaching is a way to connect employees, to signal to them that they are valued, and to support them through change and transitions.

Us: What is it like to participate in group coaching?

Dr O'Malley: One of my current clients often likens the experience to a "float spa." It is a space to pause, breathe, heighten one's awareness, and safely reflect on what is going on. So there's that AND a powerful peer-learning component!

Us: How do you use your coaching skills of noticing, listening, and asking questions in group coaching?

Dr. O'Malley: It feels particularly important to distinguish coaching from training here. I don't have specific learning objectives I seek to accomplish during each session, nor is it appropriate to seek to impart a "right" way of being. I savor silence and offer observations with permission and without attachment. I often observe members of the group adopting coach-like behaviors with one another, as well.

Us: Ali, in your experience, how does participating in group coaching impact leaders' well-being and experience at work?

Dr. O'Malley: Perceived organizational support and social support are huge here. Group coaching members realize that they are not alone and appreciate the space to slow down and reflect in the midst of intense workdays. I also see ripple effects that go beyond the members themselves. It's quite powerful to think of several dozen leaders simultaneously building self-awareness, setting and sharing specific intentions to shift their behavior, enlisting support from their leaders, and offering more support to their teams.

Team coaching

Teams are distinct entities from the individuals that comprise them,[27] and team performance is more than the sum of its parts. The interaction among team members and the context in which they operate (e.g., organizational factors) also impact team outcomes. This is what gave rise to the sub-field of team coaching. The philosophy behind team coaching is that for the team to improve, the team must be coached in the context of operating as a team; optimal levels of team effectiveness cannot be achieved solely by coaching each team member separately. For example, in one study, individual coaching for senior executives did nothing to improve the performance of the team as a whole. Only when the team was coached as a whole – with all its interpersonal dynamics, conflicts, and strong personalities – did performance of the team get stronger.[28] Team coaching focuses on the team, assuming that the whole is different and more complex than each of the individual members on their own. Team coaching has roots in consulting, organizational development, and team facilitation and training. Many of its principles are grounded in team research rather than specific to coaching.

Although there are multiple models of team coaching, it generally involves real work, in real time, to drive toward real results. In team coaching, the coach acts as a guide by asking questions and sharing observations and data, and may also weave in elements of team facilitation, training, team building, consulting, and coaching in service of the team's goals as appropriate. Team coaching entails intervening in the natural process of teams doing their work to prompt reflection, generate awareness, and encourage learning. These interventions must address not only the team's interpersonal relationships, but also the work they must accomplish together. Like individual coaching, team coaching leverages reflection and dialogue to raise awareness and surface ideas and concerns.[29] Ideally, through the experience of team coaching, individual team members develop their own ability to self-coach and problem solve. This is one important distinction from team facilitation,[30] where the facilitator leads the team in conversation toward a desired end. In team coaching, the coach draws out team members, supports them in problem solving and shifting their mindsets, and is open to how the work and conversation may unfold and evolve. Team interventions that focus solely on improving interpersonal relationships have not been shown to increase overall team performance.[31] Team coaching can include a wide range of actions: clarifying team boundaries; creating or clarifying behavioral norms; capturing unique and shared knowledge; calling out team members who violate norms; complementing the team when it is working well; teaching team members how to listen; and having the team take a break to reflect on how the team is doing. The key is that whether it's a sports team preparing for a big game or a high-performance team with responsibility for an important project, the coaching occurs within the context of the team and the work it is trying to accomplish.

Professional coaches participate in rigorous training and certification. The foundation of their training is in the skills you learned in Chapter 4: deep listening, asking questions, adopting a coaching mindset, and other capabilities highlighted in the International Coaching Federation (ICF) competencies and similar models.[32] Coaches who practice team coaching typically invest in further capability building. Team coaching is not for the faint of heart: really noticing and working with all the individual personalities and group dynamics in a team coaching setting is challenging. Additional education on team dynamics and effective strategies for engaging with team members can help a professional coach build their skill set and be ready for team coaching opportunities.

Throughout this chapter we highlighted ways in which coaching can be used to increase the functioning of groups and teams. They can be applied in any level of formality to impact yourself in relation to others, how you experience interpersonal dynamics and how to shift them. In Chapter 6 we look beyond groups and teams, to further levels of aggregation, to examine how coaching mindsets and skills can influence organizations. Coaching tends to show up in predictable ways in organizations and can influence the culture, climate, and even policies therein. Approaching organizational system design with a coaching mindset can create more empowered and purposeful organizations.

Chapter 5 Key idea

Powerful interpersonal dynamics are at play in group and team settings, and leader and team member use of coaching skills can unlock high performance and create a psychologically safe, healthy culture

Want to learn more? Check out

The Team Coaching Podcast: https://teamcoachingzone.com/team-coaching-podcast produced by the Team Coaching Zone and is available on Apple Podcasts, YouTube, Spotify, Stitcher, and Google Podcasts. Dr. Krister Lowe and Carissa Bub explore the art and science of team coaching.

This *Harvard Business Review* article on collaborative overload: https://hbr.org/2016/01/collaborative-overload

Recommended reading

Coaching the team at work by David Clutterbuck

The culture code by Daniel Coyle

Diversity, inclusion, and belonging in coaching: a practical guide by Salma Shah

Humble inquiry by Edgar Schein

The inner work of racial justice by Rhonda V. Magee

Notes

1 Hackman, J. (2009). Why teams don't work. Interview by Diane Coutu. *Harvard business review*, 87, 98–105, 130.
2 Harari, Y. N. (2014). *Sapiens: A brief history of humankind*. New York: Harper, Random House.
3 Edmondson, A. C., Dillon, J. R., & Roloff, K. S. (2007). Three perspectives on team learning: Outcome improvement, task mastery, and group process. *The Academy of Management Annals, 1*(1), 269–314. https://doi.org/10.5465/078559811
   Cohen, S. G., & Bailey, D. E. (1997). What makes teams work: Group effectiveness research from the shop floor to the executive suite. *Journal of Management, 23*(3), 239–290. https://doi.org/10.1177/014920639702300303
4 Gagné, M., & Deci, E. L. (2005). Self-determination theory and work motivation. *Journal of Organizational Behavior, 26*(4), 331–362. https://doi.org/10.1002/job.322
   Maslow, A. H. (1971). *The farther reaches of human nature* (Vol. 19711). New York, NY: Viking Press.
   Colquitt, A. L. (2017). *Next generation performance management: The triumph of science over myth and superstition*. Charlotte, NC: Information Age Publishing Inc.
5 CEB Corporate Leadership Council. (2012). *Driving breakthrough performance in the new work environment*. Arlington, VA: Author.
6 Cross, R., Rebele, R., & Grant, A. (2016, January–February). Collaborative overload. *Harvard Business Review*. https://hbr.org/2016/01/collaborative-overload
7 Lencioni, P. (2002). *The five dysfunctions of a team: A leadership fable*. Jossey-Bass.
8 Hougaard, R., Carter, J., Brewerton, V., & Pladevall, J. (2018). Why do so many managers forget they're human beings?. *Harvard Business Review*. https://hbr.org/2018/01/why-do-so-many-managers-forget-theyre-human-beings
9 Barsade, S. G. (2002). The ripple effect: Emotional contagion and its influence on group behavior. *Administrative Science Quarterly, 47*(4), 644–675. https://doi.org/10.2307/3094912
10 Hatfield, E., Cacioppo, J. T., & Rapson, R. L. (1993). Emotional contagion. *Current Directions in Psychological Science, 2*(3), 96–100. https://doi.org/10.1111/1467-8721.ep10770953

11 Jeannotte, A., Eatough, E., & Kellerman, G. R. (2020). Resilience in an age of uncertainty: Cultivating resilient leaders, teams, and organizations. *BetterUp* [Report]. https://grow.betterup.com/resilience

12 Dierdorff, E. C., Fisher, D. M., & Rubin, R. S. (2019). The power of percipience: Consequences of self-awareness in teams on team-level functioning and performance. *Journal of Management, 45*(7), 2891–2919. https://doi.org/10.1177/0149206318774622

13 Totterdell, P. (2000). Catching moods and hitting runs: Mood linkage and subjective performance in professional sport teams. *Journal of Applied Psychology, 85*(6), 848–859. https://doi.org/10.1037/0021-9010.85.6.848

14 Barsade. (2002). The ripple effect. 96–100.

15 Hackman. (2009). Teams.

16 Hackman. (2009). Teams.

17 Porter, J. (2019, January 29). To improve your team, first work on yourself. *Harvard Business Review.* https://hbr.org/2019/01/to-improve-your-team-first-work-on-yourself

18 Lawrence, E., Dunn, M. W., & Weisfeld-Spolter, S. (2018). Developing leadership potential in graduate students with assessment, self-awareness, reflection and coaching. *Journal of Management Development, 37*(8), 634–651. https://doi.org/10.1108/JMD-11-2017-0390

19 Chow, G. M., & Luzzeri, M. (2019). Post-event reflection: A tool to facilitate self-awareness, self-monitoring, and self-regulation in athletes. *Journal of Sport Psychology in Action, 10*(2), 106–118. https://doi.org/10.1080/21520704.2018.1555565

20 Ardelt, M., & Grunwald, S. (2018). The importance of self-reflection and awareness for human development in hard times. *Research in Human Development, 15*(3–4), 187–199. https://doi.org/10.1080/15427609.2018.1489098

21 Gartner. (2021, May 25). *Gartner HR research shows organizations must reinvent their employee value proposition to deliver a more human deal* [Press Release]. www.gartner.com/en/newsroom/press-releases/2020-05-25-gartner-hr-research-shows-organizations-must-reinvent-their-employment-value-proposition-to-deliver-a-more-human-deal

22 Eatough, E. (2021, December 15). Think your employees feel equally comfortable at work? Think again. *BetterUp.* www.betterup.com/blog/think-your-employees-feel-equally-comfortable-at-work-think-again#:~:text=Team%20Culture%20Perceptions%20by%20Group%20Identity&text=That%20data%20revealed%20that%20URGs,jobs%20and%20have%20lower%20productivity.

23 Shah, S. (2022). *Diversity, inclusion and belonging in coaching: A practical guide.* London: Kogan Page Publishers.

24 Petrocelli, J. V. (2002). Effectiveness of group cognitive-behavioral therapy for general symptomatology: A meta-analysis. *Journal for Specialists in Group Work, 27*(1), 92–115. https://doi.org/10.1177/0193392202027001008

25 Mühlberger, M. D., & Traut-Mattausch, E. (2015). Leading to effectiveness: Comparing dyadic coaching and group coaching. *Journal of Applied Behavioral Science, 51*(2), 198–230. https://doi.org/10.1177/0021886315574331

26 Mallinckrodt, B. (1989). Social support and the effectiveness of group therapy. *Journal of Counseling Psychology, 36*(2), 170–175. https://doi.org/10.1037/0022-0167.36.2.170

27 Wageman, R., Nunes, D. A., Burruss, J. A., & Hackman, J. R. (2008). *Senior leadership teams: What it takes to make them great.* Boston: Harvard Business Review Press.

28 Hackman. (2009). Teams.

29 Clutterbuck, D. (2009). *Coaching the team at work.* London: Nicholas Brealey International.

30 Hicks, B. (2010). *Team coaching: A literature review.* Brighton, UK: Institute for Employment Studies. www.employment-studies.co.uk/system/files/resources/files/mp88.pdf

31 Kaplan, R. E. (1979). The conspicuous absence of evidence that process consultation enhances task performance. *The Journal of Applied Behavioral Science, 15*(3), 346–360. https://doi.org/10.1177/002188637901500309

   Salas, E., Rozell, D., Mullen, B., & Driskell, J. E. (1999). The effect of team building on performance: An integration. *Small Group Research, 30*(3), 309–329. https://doi.org/10.1177/104649649903000303

   Hackman, J. R., & Wageman, R. (2005). A theory of team coaching. *Academy of Management Review, 30*(2), 269–287. https://doi.org/10.5465/amr.2005.16387885

32 International Coaching Federation. (2021). *ICF core competencies.* https://coachfederation.org/core-competencies

Part 3

Your coaching impact

In Part 2, we introduced coaching skills and discussed how they can be used to improve your interactions with other people – whether it be in 1:1 relationships (Chapter 4) or within groups and teams (Chapter 5). In Part 3, we apply coaching skills and mindsets to more complex interpersonal interactions. We believe that having a coaching mindset and practicing coaching skills can also shift the way organizations (Chapter 6) and even societies (Chapter 7) function. We'll talk about the traditional ways coaching tends to show up in organizations, but we'll also talk about the less obvious ways it can be used to impact organizational systems. We'll then turn to a bigger stage yet – society and the world more broadly. We'll tackle how a coaching mindset and skill set can not only help with some of your most meaningful roles outside of work (e.g., as a parent/caretaker) but also address some of the world's most pervasive challenges – racism, sexism, political polarization, climate change, and beyond.

DOI: 10.4324/9781003166917-8

6
Applying your coaching approach in organizations

Questions we'll answer in this chapter:

1. How do organizations use coaching?
2. What impact can coaching have at the organizational level?
3. How can coaching enhance organizational practices?

In the last company-wide meeting, the CEO of a large, national food production company announced they'd be making some changes to maintain a competitive edge. These included changes to organizational structure, a new performance management process, a new set of company values, and expectations for specific behaviors to support the changes. One of the new values being adopted was *innovation*, which the CEO emphasized is critical for the company to continue to grow and keep up with competitors.

After the meeting, the "water cooler talk" struck a cynical tone. "Every idea I've raised has been shot down. They don't want to do anything that isn't *the way we've always done it*," Priyanka said. "I know what you mean," Rob replied. "Last year I was responsible for a pilot that was intended to break new ground. When we didn't hit the targets, my performance rating reflected it – and my bonus. That's the *last* time I raise my hand to venture into the unknown."

Priyanka wanted to try new things but felt like she was running into institutional resistance. Meanwhile, Rob was in a position to try new things, but at what felt like personal cost. They both understood why innovation was being added to the company values. They even shared that value on an individual level. Yet, they hadn't seen that value reinforced behaviorally by leadership or encouraged by systems and processes within the organization. They felt like the organization lacked a genuine desire to innovate. Priyanka and Rob felt like the new value was going to be something on the website

DOI: 10.4324/9781003166917-9

but little more. As time went on, there were two types of conversations going on in the company: (1) the conversations that were happening *during* the meeting (encouraging innovation) and (2) the conversations that were happening *after* the meeting (cynicism and skepticism).

Elody was a vice president in the company's operations group. She was getting pressure from her leadership that they weren't being bold enough or moving fast enough. In every team meeting, she was dutifully hitting home the innovation message – why it is critical for the business and how every member of the organization has a responsibility to contribute. She fully understood why they needed to modernize. She didn't disagree with the direction at all and was even excited for the opportunity to replace things that they'd long known were sub-optimized. That said, she knew the realities of the business. At the end of the day, switching from something that might be less than optimal to something new (i.e., something that might not work) meant risk. She worried about the implications of that risk on her team, the business, and, if she was honest with herself, the implications for her own career. As a result, she stayed closely and personally involved in any new initiatives and had no tolerance for mistakes. She pushed the team to think more creatively and offered clear and direct solutions when she saw them getting stuck.

When Elody received the results from her function's most recent culture survey, she was surprised and disappointed. The survey indicated that people in her function felt micromanaged and afraid to speak up. Their innovation scores were lower than ever, and burnout was higher than ever. She didn't understand what she was doing wrong. She felt like she was working hard to do what the company needed, but it only seemed to make things worse.

People, culture, and behavior change

Organizations maintain competitive advantage by building capabilities to meet customer needs. All organizational capabilities are either composed of, or implemented through, people. Even highly automated industries and businesses still have people behind each of those robots. Whether it's executing on an existing strategy and goals or changing to meet new demands, people working in organizations need to understand and embrace the vision and direction, and they need to have the capacity and resources to deliver, in order for those aspirations to be realized. The most effective organizations connect business strategy to organizational culture, all the way down to individual behavior. This kind of alignment sounds straightforward – a clear strategy, communicated and modeled by leadership, and reinforced by organizational systems and processes (who and how they hire, promote, develop, and reward). However, what appears simple and straightforward on paper can be messy in practice.

In previous chapters, we've built the mental image of each of us as an iceberg and described the complexity that arises as more people (and icebergs) get introduced. Edgar Schein,[1] one of the foremost experts on organizational culture, adopted a metaphor of a lily pond to describe culture as an ecosystem that includes what we see at the surface, as well as what runs deep beneath the surface. He defines culture as the sum total of everything an organization has learned in its history in dealing with the external problems – which would be goals, strategy, how we do things – and how it organizes itself internally. Not unlike the iceberg model, Schein's concept of organizational culture as a lily pond suggests that there are outward, visible elements that we see (e.g., symbols, norms) – like the lily pads and blossoms that we see at the surface of a pond. Below the surface are the stems of each of those lilies, which represent less visible elements, such as mindsets, power dynamics, and relationships. Further beneath the surface, in the bed of the lily pond, are the roots of the plants, which symbolize emotions and motivations of people within the organization. If the roots are not healthy and strong, the stems, leaves, buds, and blossoms of the lily will suffer; the health of the entire ecosystem depends on what is happening deep beneath the surface – not only in the water, but deep in the soil.

Other researchers describe organizational culture and climate as being "absorbed by people through their everyday experiences and daily interactions with others; they serve as implicit roadmaps for daily life."[2] These roadmaps serve a very practical function for employees in that they help people focus and provide guidelines on how to behave. Individual-level change is always hard to sustain, but without structural change to reinforce it, it can be nearly impossible. This means that an organization's culture can either support and reinforce or work *against* its explicit change goals. When there's a gap between the culture and the goals, the organization needs to adjust the goal or adjust the culture. Organizations can make changes to strategy, structure, and systems to drive and sustain impact. Those things are the more tangible manifestations of culture and can be more satisfying to take on as part of a transformation initiative. They're easier to define, change, and mark progress around. In contrast, as we learned from Schein, culture is always something that has been learned, with deep and complex roots, making it difficult to change. Changing strategy, structure, and systems without addressing the cultural roots that gave rise to and sustained them in the first place is like cutting the top of the bamboo stalk rather than pulling it out by its root – it will just continue to grow back.

Enter coaching

Two of the biggest barriers to successfully transforming culture and strategy in organizations are engendering commitment and maintaining momentum among the people within the organization. These barriers might sound familiar, as they show up at the individual level too. Change requires a holistic suite of well-choreographed approaches. If it's hard to change one person's behavior, changing the behavior of a whole organization is exponentially harder. Take our example at the start of the chapter. During the company-wide meeting, everyone seemed to embrace the new company value of innovation. And in private settings, members of that organization – like Priyanka and Rob – felt cynical and unsupportive of the proposed changes. Elody embraced the change but failed to adopt the right set of behaviors to enable increased innovation in her team. Leaders often need coaching or other forms of support to lead through change. Leading change requires a huge infusion of time and resources, and the ability to overcome fear, fatigue, and resistance amidst a sea of constant change (their own and that of those around them), day after day. It requires the ability to identify gaps and obstructions between "as is" (current state) and "to be" (the desired state or goal) – a process that's often guided by a consultant, coach, or facilitator.[3] The final mile – shifting the behaviors, values, assumptions, and mindsets of the entire employee population – is often neglected and is a place where coaching can help. In previous chapters, we described how and why coaching can help you and those around you be more effective in accomplishing your goals and working together more effectively. In this chapter, we extend those concepts to the organizational level. We break the mechanisms down into leadership, culture, and policies and practices.

Leadership

Leaders have a disproportionate role in creating and shaping culture. During times of intentional change, leaders' support, actions, and sense of accountability can make or break the success of that change. Leaders must paint a vision for the future and articulate why the current state would no longer allow them to achieve that future. But just as Priyanka and Rob's comments reflected, messaging is not transformation – or even change. Leaders must also model changes through behavior: what they do; who they hire, fire, and promote; what they spend their time on; and how they talk about and measure success. However, the average employee has little day-to-day contact with senior leaders. So, while transformation starts at the top, it only happens when the frontline and their managers make behavioral shifts. This means that leaders at every level need to be brought along to ensure that the day-to-day interactions an employee has are consistent with the culture required to enable the organization's strategy.

Coaching can help leaders navigate and lead through change by helping them develop their cognitive agility, stress management, problem solving, communication skills, and ability to build trust and psychological safety. In addition, a growing number of studies indicate that executive coaching has positive effects on the resilience of managers during organizational transformation efforts.[4] Further, as leaders throughout the organization receive coaching, there is a positive ripple effect on their teams[5] due to their own growth but also because they can improve their own coaching skills and pay it forward. In other words, to successfully lead change, leaders usually need to change some of their *own* mindsets, beliefs, and behaviors. As you know from earlier chapters in this book, coaching can help with all of those! And, particularly in the case of Elody, developing and using their coaching skills can help leaders lead that change more effectively and successfully bring others along with them. Let's have some empathy for Elody; her intentions are in the right place. She sees the importance in the change. She is trying so hard to support that change and drive innovation in her team. And . . . she is doing a lot of things wrong.

Let's imagine a positive twist in this example.

Elody sits down to talk with her HR business partner, Corey: "I feel like I'm running on a hamster wheel. Or maybe banging my head against a wall. I don't know what the right metaphor is, but I am trying hard to push my team to be innovative, but they aren't changing, and now I get these terrible survey results. I'm at a loss for what to do next."

Lucky for Elody, Corey has a fine set of coaching skills. They listen intently to Elody, noticing her tone, emotions, and how worn out and defeated she appears.

Corey affirms Elody: "Elody, I can see that you are working hard on this. And I can also see where you feel defeated and don't know what to do next."

Simply from feeling seen and heard, Elody relaxes and lets out a deep exhale.

Corey smiles and sees an opening: "Elody, tell me more about what you've been trying that doesn't seem to be working."

"I'm beating this drum of innovation over and over. I can't possibly say it more than I already am. I am telling my team to be more innovative and think more creatively. They aren't, so I'm giving them clear direction on what they need to be doing to solve some of these operations challenges. It's gotten to the point where I've had to ask them to CC me on every email on certain projects, and I join every project call. I am investing so much time and energy in this and it's going nowhere," Elody exclaims.

Corey paraphrases back to Elody what they heard, and checks with Elody for accuracy. Corey follows with a question: "Elody, I remember that you were involved in developing and launching that zero-waste compost project several years ago. What an amazing success that project has been. That seems to me like a great example of innovation in our company. What was different about that project?"

Elody nods enthusiastically and pauses to reflect. "Corey – great point. That project was out of character for us in terms of innovation and has had a great impact. Kareem was my leader on that initiative. I sure do miss him."

"What was it like working with Kareen on that initiative?" Corey asks.

Elody smiles and laughs. "I see where you are going with this Corey. Kareem basically did the OPPOSITE of everything I'm doing. We made a TON of mistakes in the early stages of that project. He had this great balance of creating a vision and making us feel safe and supported but let us sort of run with it."

Corey smiles and listens intently to Elody.

Elody continues, "I feel like I have a vice grip on this project. I feel so much tension and I know my team must feel it, too. I know I need to change the way I'm approaching this with my team. It's funny – I feel so tired just think-ing about it, and I also know it's the right thing to do."

Over the next 20 minutes, Corey continues to listen deeply to Elody and raise simple, helpful questions to support her in thinking through what she wants to try differently with her team. Elody leaves the conversation with a plan to directly address her new approach with leaders on her team. She commits to noticing when she's about to tell people what to do and instead ask them a question to support them in coming up with the solution. She thinks through ways that she can shield and support her team so that they feel safe taking risks and making mistakes.

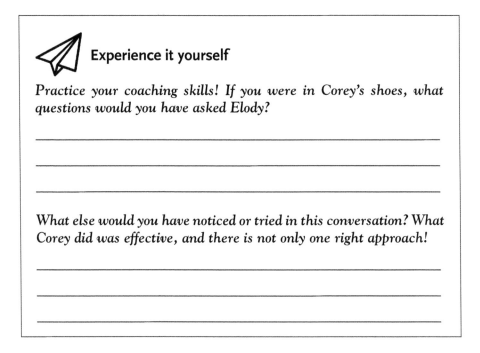

Experience it yourself

Practice your coaching skills! If you were in Corey's shoes, what questions would you have asked Elody?

_____

_____

_____

What else would you have noticed or tried in this conversation? What Corey did was effective, and there is not only one right approach!

_____

_____

_____

In this example, Elody benefited from Corey's coaching skills of deep lis-tening, noticing, and asking helpful questions. Corey provided no advice or direction to Elody, but instead used their coaching skills to raise Elody's awareness and identify new behaviors she wants to try out with her team, including using some coaching skills herself (asking her team questions rather than giving them a solution). This conversation is reminiscent of what you read about using coaching skills in 1:1 interactions in Chapter 4. And yet, the context of this conversation is relevant here in Chapter 6: supporting a leader in navigating change effectively with her team. Elody was fortunate to have an HR business partner with such strong coaching skills. But that's not always the case. If Elody had not been able to count on Corey, she could have found coaching support in a few other ways, such as her manager (assuming they have a robust coaching skill set), an internal professional coach, or even an external professional coach. Though the focus of this book is on a coaching mindset and skill set that anyone can develop and use, in this next section we will dip a toe into the world of professional coaching.

Formal coaching practices in organizations

Organizations use coaching in myriad ways, ranging from totally ad hoc and/ or informal to formal, structured programs (and we should acknowledge that for some organizations their use of coaching is "not at all" – something we hope they will remedy!). And, as we noted above, coaching can take many forms in an organization. HR practitioners and managers can develop and use their coaching skill set with direct reports or internal clients. Employees of all tenures and roles can develop their coaching skills to have better interactions with peers and cross-functional team members. Increasingly, organizations are developing internal coaching practices where professional coaches are either hired or trained to work with leaders throughout the organization. And organizations' use of external professional coaches continues to increase year over year, with the industry seeing between roughly 7% growth annually.[6]

In this next section, we explore at what coaching practices in organizations can look like, starting with a maturity model of coaching in organizations. In this model we draw on the work of coaches and coaching researchers/ thought leaders, David Peterson[7] and Jeremy Stover,[8] with a few adaptations based on our own work. The idea behind this maturity model of coaching is that organizations progress through a series of stages as they become more intentional in their use of coaching/coaches and more focused on delivering return-on-investment (ROI). As such strategic focus tends to increase, so does the focus on measuring results.

The first stage is *Ad hoc*. In this stage coaching is applied reactively in response to requests or situations. There may be no central point of management, contact, or oversight in an organization that takes an ad hoc approach. In other words, if a leader decides they want a coach, they try to find some support and budget for it and might even find their own coach. Leaders may get little or no guidance on when or why they may want to work with a coach. Coaching is seen as a high-touch solution for needs like supporting a new executive in their onboarding or retaining a high-potential employee who feels stagnant in her role. Organizations that are providing coaching in this way are signaling a belief that coaching is effective – at least under certain circumstances.

The second stage of maturity is *Managed* coaching. In this stage, coaching is "champion-driven": an individual within the organization has been appointed to oversee or consolidate coaching. Organizations at this level of maturity are generally beginning to establish coach selection criteria, screen and keep track of coaches and coaching engagements, define the coaching process, and measure participant reactions to coaching. By starting to centralize coaching investments, the organization can also better identify patterns of need, identify what's working and what's not, and use those learnings to make further investment decisions.

We refer to the third stage as *Proactive*. In organizations at the Proactive stage of maturity, coaching investments are made in targeted groups to address a specific organizational need. Organizations in this stage are likely to focus on developing talent pools to generate organizational and individual value. For example, an intake process may be used to ensure that coaching is truly the appropriate solution for the individual seeking coaching. In our (Brodie & Shonna's) experience with people and talent processes, people often start with a solution, rather than getting clear on the problem or the need. Someone comes to their HR business partner or talent partner and says, "I need coaching," rather than starting with what challenge they are facing and what they are looking to achieve. Training, therapy, mentoring, feedback, a better manager, or a vacation might actually be the solution, depending on what problem they are looking to solve. Proactive management of coaching activity tends to result in an increased strategic focus on who provides and who receives coaching. A proactive approach may also include a focus on creating a coaching culture and an increased focus on ROI.

The fourth and among the most mature stages is *Strategic*. Coaching investments in this stage are driven by organizational talent strategy. Companies identify pivotal talent pools and provide optimal development to those pools to build individual and organizational capability. Targeting specific groups is often associated with having specific outcomes in mind for the coaching, such as investing in diverse leaders to increase diversity in the talent pipeline or using coaching as a complement to a high-potential leader development program. The organization may work with several coaching providers who can meet specific needs – such as firms that specialize in communication or executive presence or firms that have a global footprint and can bring a consistent approach to coaching leaders around the globe. This typically involves more systematic tracking of relationship between talent development and business key performance indicators (KPIs).

BetterUp added one more stage to the maturity model that we refer to as *Adaptive*. There are several similarities between strategic and adaptive in the sense that the focus is on optimizing development, which may or may not be coaching at a particular time and includes systematic tracking of outcomes. A key difference, however, is that optimization shifts from group attributes (e.g., a particular role) to the individual level (e.g., coaching readiness, motivation, transitions). This sounds far-fetched, particularly at scale for a large organization, but new models for coaching (e.g., virtual coaching through a technology platform) combined with advances in technology (e.g., machine learning) have created a pathway to achieve precision-development.[9] This means that in the future, it is likely feasible that organizations will rely on technology that can not only help them to align coaching to specific populations in service of organizational goals, but also to match the right intervention for each person and their goals at a given point of time and adapt over time.

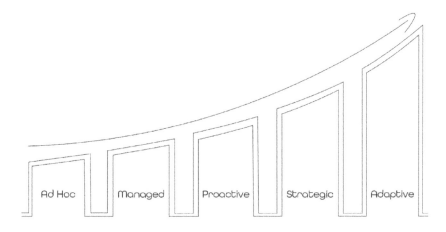

Ad Hoc   Managed   Proactive   Strategic   Adaptive

Who provides coaching?

Just as there are a variety of approaches and philosophies that organizations employ in deciding who gets coaching, there are a number of models to choose from regarding who provides coaching. We've continually argued that anyone, in any role, can use coaching skills and see a positive impact. That said, there are pros and cons inherent in any role if the goal is to be of service to the other person. In Table 6.1, we outline the pros and cons of five different roles for providing coaching: direct managers, HR colleagues (such as an HR or talent business partner), peers, internal professional coaches, and external professional coaches. One key distinction between the manager, HR colleague, and peer versus the internal and external professional coach is that the former three bring their coaching skill set to the conversation – they are likely *not* professionally trained and certified coaches. On the other hand, the internal and external professional coaches have presumably gone through rigorous training and certification, and coaching is a focal part of their "day job." As you'll see, there are advantages and disadvantages to each, and the right solution depends on the situation.

Let's go back to our story with Priyanka and Rob. "Every idea I've raised has been shot down. They don't want to do anything that isn't the way we've always done it," Priyanka said. This time, instead of commiserating, Rob puts on his peer coach hat. "What do you make of that?" Rob asks curiously.

Priyanka replies, "I'm not sure. I just don't think they're serious about wanting to innovate."

Rob pauses for a moment, then asks, "Priyanka, when you say 'they,' who do you have in mind?"

Priyanka gets an inquisitive look on her face, thinks for a moment, then says, "Well I guess the person I really have in mind is my manager. I sometimes see him as the face of 'the company.' And now that I think of it, I haven't really talked to him directly about it."

Rob draws out more: "What do you mean?"

"The situations that I have in mind were in team meetings – I try to throw out ideas and get the creative juices flowing and have often felt like my ideas are discounted or shot down in those meetings," Priyanka shares. "But I can see now that my manager might think I'm just throwing things at the wall; these meetings probably aren't the best forum to have a real conversation about my ideas."

Rob asks, "What would be a better forum?"

Priyanka has on her best thinking face and nods, "Yeah . . . I need to bring these to my manager directly in our 1:1s. And let him know these are real ideas, not half-baked suggestions I'm just throwing out at team meetings."

Table 6.1 Pros and cons of five different roles for providing coaching

Who provides coaching?	*Pros*	*Cons*
Manager	• Direct visibility into the individual's performance and direct access to input from others • In an ideal position to provide performance coaching • Knows the business, culture, and context • Has formal authority and control over resources, decisions, etc. • Can occur organically and not require a formal program • Low to no cost (e.g., part of manager's role)	• What's best for the individual and what's best for the company (or manager) may be in conflict • Co-ownership of outcomes can impact actual or perceived conflicts of interest, reducing trust • Variability in skill sets (how effective are their coaching skills?) • Time constraints depending on scope of the manager's role and responsibilities • Performance vs. development environment (see appendix) • Nature of the relationship – team members are rarely able to choose their manager
HR colleague	• May already have visibility into the individual's work, challenges, and relationships • May be skilled in the development of others • Aware of other people, talent tools, and resources available • Knows the business, culture, and context • Can occur organically and not require a formal program • Low to no cost	• What's best for the individual and what's best for the company may be in conflict • May be having similar conversations with the individual's manager or peers and therefore lack objectivity • May be required to act on certain pieces of information that are shared, even if confidentiality is assumed • Variability in depth and quality of coaching skills • Variability in levels of trust between employees and HR • May devolve into venting or complaining

Who provides coaching?	Pros	Cons
Peer	• Provides an opportunity for mutual learning • Can provide other benefits, such as networking, practicing coaching skills, and providing social support • Generally know the business, culture, and context • Can occur organically or be part of a peer-coaching program • Low to no cost	• Training and ongoing coaching skill development must be provided • Maintaining consistency • Typically not trained to specialize in the development of others • More challenging to stay objective due to familiarity and internal pressures • Availability can be limited due to other responsibilities or priorities • Administrative overhead required for formal peer-coaching programs • Potential for devolving into mentoring, venting, or complaining
Internal professional coach	• Depending on who they are and how they are sourced, they generally know the business, culture, and context • They can be less expensive than external coaches, depending on the staffing model • Are professionally trained and bring a high-caliber coaching approach • More objective than a manager or peer	• More challenging to stay objective due to familiarity and internal pressures • Typically have multiple relationships either professionally or through multiple coaching engagements that can create actual or perceived conflicts of interest, impacting trust • Availability can be limited, depending on scope of internal coaching practice • May require significant administrative overhead

(*Continued*)

Table 6.1 (Continued)

Who provides coaching?	Pros	Cons
External professional coach	• More impartial and less affected by internal politics, creating greater trust • Often more extensive or specialist skill sets • Outside perspectives from working with a range of clients • Dedicated and tailored support depending on the individual's needs • Objective and unencumbered by pre-existing knowledge or agendas	• Need to be onboarded to business, culture, and context • Can be costly, depending on model and scope of service • May provide the organization with less control over the content of the coaching and associated data • May require dedicated contact person in the organization to procure and manage coaching engagements

From here, Rob could continue to support Priyanka in thinking through when she will bring it up with her manager and even offer to help her role play the conversation. Often a peer might respond to another peer's frustration by commiserating or going straight to problem solving. By seeing an opening (more to come on this in Chapter 7!) to engage in a peer-coaching conversation, Rob can help Priyanka shift out of her feelings of frustration and even help the management understand where things might be breaking down between the company's messaging and what employees are experiencing.

Context is an important consideration in deciding who the best person is to provide coaching. In a performance context, an individual must apply their learning and experience in practice to achieve valued outcomes.[10] The consequences of error or failure can be costly for their organization or for them personally. In contrast, a developmental context is one that supports growth of an individual in ways and to an extent they themselves determine. Safe to fail. It generally requires that the developmental relationship is completely optional, that the coach has no personal stake in coaching outcomes or formal authority over the client, that the client drives the coaching agenda and leads the exploration and development of goals, desired outcomes, and measures of success. Coaching can still be effective in a performance environment; however, it's important to remember that there might be hesitance to be fully vulnerable or to take the kind of risks that might feel safer in a development context. This is one of the reasons that organizations bring in external mentors and coaches or send employees to vendor trainings. Organizations that want to be deliberately developmental have to be very intentional about ensuring the culture and climate reward risk taking.

✈ Experience it yourself

If you have had exposure to coaching, who was in the coach role? What was effective – or ineffective – about that approach to coaching?

_____

_____

_____

In what roles can you apply your coaching skills?

_____

_____

_____

Applications of coaching in organizations

Culture

We've described what culture is in organizations and how important it is that culture supports the business strategy, but we haven't said what makes a *good* organizational culture. Benjamin Schneider, an organizational psychologist, summarized what he learned about studying leadership and culture during his 50-year research career.[11] Not to overly simplify his learnings, but he found that a good culture is one that is people-oriented. The organization demonstrates that they care about and for their people and there is trust at all levels of the organization. When stated that way, many of the foundational principles of coaching – incorporating and caring for the whole person, listening, curiosity, and supporting the person's potential (without judgment) – are strongly aligned to a positive organizational culture. Further, creating and sustaining a more people-centered, inclusive corporate culture requires openness, trust, and adaptability on the part of all the people in an organization. Leadership coaching can be a catalyst for the creation of a new cultural environment.[12]

Coaching, and developmental concepts more broadly, have been seeping into organizational design (e.g., *Reinventing Organizations*,[13] *An Everyone Culture*)[14] in recent years. This is often framed through two lenses. First, fostering the development of potential and career growth is critical to building the kind of positive culture that Schneider describes. People are naturally oriented toward achievement, mastery, and meaning.[15] Organizations that help employees learn and grow will develop competitive advantage through their ability to hire, retain, and engage talent. Second, organizations *need* employees to develop, particularly given the constantly changing context and nature of business. The connections between people and business outcomes have been demonstrated through decades of research and meta-analyses.[16] It is thus in an organization's best interest to ensure that it can metabolize the lessons of experience at every level. Developmental psychologists Robert Kegan and Lisa Lahey suggested that learning and striving for one's potential should be ingrained in the day-to-day work practices of every single person. They referred to this concept as a Deliberately Developmental Organization (DDO).[17] In this model, the organization itself is the primary instrument for learning and development, with more formal interventions such as workshops, courses, mentoring, and so on being additive and not the primary vehicle for learning and development.

Coaching can be used to help shift both organizational culture and individual behaviors by prompting reflection, injecting new information into the system, and providing accountability. Coaches who support leaders through culture change often begin by conducting a cultural audit to identify the "as is" state. The coach then works with the leader(s) to articulate the desired state and why it matters (often seen through the lens of a business problem).[18] The coach provides support to the leader as they identify a plan to close the gap that spans across individuals, dyads, and teams, ultimately to a systemic, organizational approach.

Organizations that have come to see the value in coaching may strive to deliberately cultivate a *coaching culture*. A coaching culture is one in which individuals throughout the organization embrace and model a coaching mindset and behaviors, which creates the conditions for continuous learning. A coaching culture is developed not just through the presence of formal coaching (although organizations that have a coaching culture may be more likely to also invest in formal coaching), but where most people use coaching as a tool to manage, influence, and communicate with each other. This style is embodied not only by managers but also by employees at every level. Coaching cultures are also characterized by a high degree of psychological safety and organizational practices that reinforce coaching behaviors. As a result, this kind of culture encourages informal open exchanges of information and knowledge, and individuals are willing to discuss challenges and concerns and evaluate appropriate actions. Organizations with strong coaching cultures are also more likely to have higher levels of employee engagement, as well as desirable outcomes like higher productivity and performance, higher customer satisfaction, and accelerated growth and market share.

Regardless of role, every member in an organization can contribute to fostering a coaching culture by embodying a coaching mindset and skills. A coaching culture can develop both top-down, with policies, expectations and tone set from leadership, and bottom-up, based on the day-to-day behaviors of every individual in the organization. In their book chapter on developing a coaching culture, Arias and colleagues[19] outline a five-step process for organizations to intentionally invest in cultivating a coaching culture: assess, develop, implement, evaluate, and connect. In the Assess step (step 1), organizations (likely someone in the people function) undertake a gap analysis to understand the current state of their coaching culture, the goal state, and the distance between the two. This step is helpful not only for understanding the current situation, but also for articulating a vision for the future of the culture. In step 2, Develop, the organization outlines a strategy for coaching that cuts across the organization and includes coaching practices ranging from use of external coaches, to upskilling leaders, employees, and HR colleagues on coaching skills, to peer-coaching programs and even mentoring. Step 3 (Implement) is the most time and labor intensive, as it entails bringing that strategy to life by hiring internal and external coaches, bringing in or developing coaching skill learning programs, equipping individuals across the organization to coach, setting expectations for using those coaching skills, and ensuring that other people, processes, and systems support – rather than undermine – a coaching culture, among other things! This step is likely intertwined with step 4, Evaluate, as the organization gauges progress along the way according to pre-established metrics, which may include number of leaders trained on coaching skills, annual spend on external coaches, number of coaching engagements, impact of coaching engagements, key indicators on the annual employee engagement survey, and so on. Finally, step 5 (Connect) takes that measurement to the next level, with a focus on linking coaching strategy and practices to critical outcomes, such as retention, individual and organizational performance, and more. Determining causation in people practices is challenging. In other words, if an organization spent the last three years cultivating a coaching culture and then experienced record levels of retention, higher levels of engagement, and 25% growth, how much of that can be attributed to the coaching culture, versus other internal and external factors? HR and talent practitioners have become increasingly sophisticated in their use of analytics and in their ability to make causal links between people practices and critical outcomes, making this fifth step in cultivating a coaching culture challenging, but not unreachable.

In their discussion of cultivating a coaching culture, Arias and colleagues also note the risk of having conflicting processes and practices. For example, they cite performance management processes. If an organization's performance management process rewards and drives competition over collaboration, this could drive behavior that is at odds with a coaching culture. Cultures that do not tolerate mistakes and risk taking may stifle the openness, vulnerability, and curiosity needed to develop a coaching culture: if employees are afraid to ask questions or admit that they don't know the answer, they may fear repercussions rather than being open to exploration. In the section below we take a closer look at organizational processes that touch, complement, or undermine coaching behaviors.

Coaching within organizational practices

The organization's culture provides the foundation for its climate – the tactics, strategy implementation, policies, practices, and processes that point employees to the more immediate company goals and what they should focus on.[20] These tools serve as controls that help direct behavior toward the company's strategic objectives. They include things like onboarding, performance management, leadership development, career development, learning and training, outplacement, and diversity, equity, and inclusion policies and practices. Controls can be described as coercive or enabling.[21] Coercive control is the typical foundation for organizational processes and includes hierarchy, chain of command, written policies and procedures, management directives, centralized decision making, and formalization. Motivating employees is generally accomplished through external means (rewards and punishments to reinforce behavior aligned with company goals). Enabling approaches are less common, more informal, and instead rely on social, psychological, and cultural/organizational mechanisms to motivate employee behavior.

Performance management

As an example, industrial psychologists Colquitt and Goldberg[22] apply this lens to performance management systems. Traditional approaches to performance management are quite bureaucratic. They occur on a prescribed schedule (often annually), a manager has sole input and discretion over a performance evaluation, and rewards are distributed to individuals. Colquitt and Goldberg describe this as a coercive control system and recommend redesigning these systems through the lens of enablement. While coercive control systems rely on hierarchy, chain of command, written policies and procedures, and centralized decision making, enabling controls rely on social, psychological, and cultural tools to influence behavior.[23] Redesigning performance management systems through the lens of enablement might result in a greater emphasis on direction, alignment, and encouragement. It would shift from evaluating the past to helping employees understand the context for their work and understand how to progress and develop in service of organizational performance.

Research Spotlight

Dr. Rose Mueller-Hanson, Author of *Transforming Performance Management to Drive Performance: An Evidence-based Roadmap*, on the role of coaching in performance management

Us: Rose, you have deep expertise on the topic of performance management, and you're also a coach. How can coaching play a role in performance management?

Dr Mueller-Hanson: You are spot on that coaching and performance management are intertwined. Performance management is not just about doing an annual review anymore – it's about encouraging ongoing conversations between employees and managers. Most organizations are looking to increase the amount of feedback and coaching throughout the year. Coaching is so valuable to these conversations because it facilitates getting the work done, empowers the employee, and strengthens the relationship between employees and managers. Coaching helps get the work done by changing the dynamic of the conversation from mere feedback (in which the manager is passing judgment on the employee's performance) to a problem-solving partnership in which the manager helps the employee uncover and resolve roadblocks to success. This empowers the employee by supporting them to identify root causes of issues and figure out how to remove them. The collaborative nature of coaching can lead to a better relationship as well where employees and managers are working together to get to a successful outcome. Coaching is fundamentally about building trust and showing genuine interest in the other person, which is the foundation for any successful relationship.

Us: In what ways is that a shift from traditional approaches to performance management?

Dr. Mueller-Hanson: In traditional performance management, there is a heavy emphasis on evaluation and feedback. In the typical annual review, the manager discusses the ratings the employee has received, provides feedback, and ideally there is a conversation about development. However, the power dynamic is one-way. The manager is supposed to be the final arbiter of the employee's performance. There may be a discussion, but the purpose is to determine if the employee is meeting expectations and perhaps dole out rewards. Most organizations are recognizing that the traditional process does little to actually improve performance and that ongoing coaching is essential to truly driving change.

Us: How can individual leaders apply their coaching skills in performance management settings? What skills are most valuable and relevant here?

Dr. Mueller-Hanson: The specific skills that are most useful are cultivating curiosity and asking powerful questions. By approaching conversations with a mindset of being curious, it leaves both parties more open to understand a situation more fully before drawing conclusions. This is so critical in performance management because traditional PM is about evaluating the performance of individuals. The truth is that performance is the result of many complex factors, some of which are outside the individual's control. By staying curious, managers and employees can dig deeper into situations and better understand what might be getting in the way of success and how to overcome it. Powerful questions are a specific way of expressing curiosity and so much more. A really powerful question can help people think about issues in new ways and develop new insights. By using questions and not statements, people learn and develop new skills, which I think is the ultimate purpose of performance management – to facilitate success through growth.

Us: Rose, what is one thing you wish people knew or would do differently when it comes to performance management?

Dr. Mueller-Hanson: Many organizations are hyper-focused on improving the feedback skills of their managers. While feedback is important, I'd argue that coaching skills are even more valuable. Feedback, by definition, is one-way. It automatically highlights the power dynamic between two people. The feedback provider is judging the performance/effectiveness/behavior of the feedback recipient. Many people fear giving and receiving feedback because they are uncomfortable with this dynamic. Training and practice can help make it easier, but for many feedback will still be difficult and awkward. There is of course a time and place for this type of feedback. However, there are many situations in which coaching may be the place to start. When things don't go as planned, starting with a coaching mindset shifts the power dynamic from boss-subordinate to partnership. If organizations are struggling to help their managers learn to provide feedback, I'd suggest focusing more heavily on coaching. It will take the pressure off managers to be performance judges and instead empower them to be performance coaches, which is a much more appealing role for most people.

Like the distinction between coercive and enabling controls, organizational policies and practices take a different shape when seen through a coaching mindset. Coaches accept others unconditionally, trust that they have the resources needed to solve their own challenges (or that others have the capacity to seek out these resources as needed), have others' long-term best interests at heart, challenge us when necessary and cheer us on, and they motivate us to get out of our own way. It recognizes no one has privileged access to the truth and that we are always co-creating our reality. Take a minute to reflect on your own experience with performance management. We'll help . . .

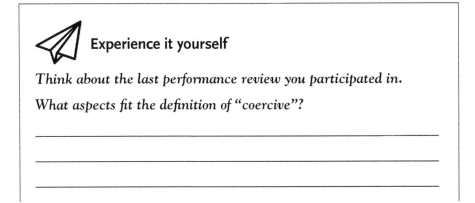

Experience it yourself

Think about the last performance review you participated in.

What aspects fit the definition of "coercive"?

_____

_____

_____

What aspects fit the definition of "enabling"?

_____

_____

_____

Reflect on your thoughts, feelings, and behaviors before and after the review. What impact did it have on you?

_____

_____

_____

Put yourself into a coaching mindset. What aspect of the process would you change? Why?

_____

_____

_____

In a shift from "standalone" annual performance reviews to an ongoing approach to performance management, many organizations have integrated coaching or a coaching approach into their process. An ongoing performance management approach focuses on frequent, informal feedback all throughout the year, with a regular cadence of check-ins between manager and employee. This is where a manager's coaching skills play a critical role. In shifting from a focus on evaluation, compensation, and legal protection to an emphasis on employee growth and development, modern approaches to performance management require managers to expand their approach from directive to more coach-like. The manager's role shifts from monitoring employees' work to supporting them and empowering them to learn and grow while delivering on the expectations of their role. To do this effectively managers must have a solid foundation in best practices for providing feedback, and this is complemented by their use of key coaching skills, like empowering their employee to problem solve and own the solution, listening, and asking generative questions. In fact, in delivering feedback to a direct report, a manager may follow with a coaching question to support the employee in making sense of the feedback and thinking about what they will do with it.

In shifting from a focus on evaluation, compensation, and legal protection to an emphasis on employee growth and development, modern approaches to performance management require managers to expand their approach from directive to more coach-like.

For example, in a quarterly check-in conversation, Abel's manager shares feedback with him about his leadership of a project team: "Abel, in your leadership of Project X, I noticed that your stakeholder communications did not come at a predictable cadence. At the start of the project, you were sending them weekly, on Friday afternoons. Over the last few months, there have been several instances where you did not send out stakeholder updates. As a result, I have gotten questions from several key stakeholders about where the project stands. You're still leading this project for the next six months. How do you want to communicate with stakeholders?" In this example, Abel's manager shares clear and direct feedback with him about his performance on Project X. He then shares an open-ended, judgment-free, curious question at the end to support Abel in thinking about how he wants to act on this feedback. Ultimately, the purpose of giving others feedback is to influence their future behavior. Asking a curious question can help the feedback recipient pause to digest the feedback and think about what they want to do with it, and why. In Abel's case, his manager may ask what he wants his relationships with stakeholders to be like, or what impression he wants to make with them.

Learning and development

Research has consistently shown that coaching boosts the impact of several learning and development activities. One tool that is frequently used for leader development is 360 feedback, where leaders receive feedback on their performance, strengths, development opportunities, specific competencies, and more as a way of holding up the mirror and enhancing their self-awareness. Working through 360 feedback with a coach leads to a variety of important outcomes. One study found that leaders who worked with a coach after receiving their 360 feedback set more specific goals, were more likely to have follow-up conversations based on the feedback, and showed greater improvements in performance, as compared to colleagues who did not work with a coach.[24] Another study found that leaders who received 360 feedback and worked with a coach to interpret the feedback and decide where to focus had higher levels of satisfaction, more commitment to their organization, reduced intention to leave the organization, and ultimately higher business performance.[25]

Working with a coach to make sense of 360 feedback is important because the quantity of feedback can feel overwhelming. When leaders are simply handed a 360 report and left to make sense of it on their own, a pattern typically emerges: They read it once, probably feel overwhelmed, maybe a little defensive. They may come back and read it again. They over-index on the negative feedback and gloss over the strengths and positive feedback. They set some vague aspirations for what they will do, then stick the report on a shelf or in a folder and soon forget about it. Certainly, there are exceptions to this pattern, but in our combined 30+ year experience as industrial-organizational psychologists and coaches, this is what we see most often. Alternatively, when leaders have the opportunity to work with a coach on their 360 feedback, the pattern unfolds very differently. The coach will support the leader in soaking up the positive feedback and reflecting on their strengths, rather than simply glossing over them to get to the negative feedback. The coach will also support the leader in identifying follow-up conversations they may want to have. Often leaders expect a 360 to be full of answers and are surprised when the feedback raises more questions. A coach can help the leader think through those questions and what they want to do with them. A coach can also support the leader in deciding what feedback to focus on for their development. Trying to work on too many development areas will set the leader up for failure; the coach will support the leader in prioritizing the top one or two opportunities to focus on first. The coach will also support the leader in setting specific goals to drive their development, and with ongoing coaching, be their accountability partner as the leader experiments with new behaviors and reflects on the impact of those behaviors. In short, the 360 feedback experience is far more effective and more likely to lead to behavior change when the leader has coaching support, either from a professional coach, a peer coach, or an HR business partner with strong coaching skills.

Coaching is also a valuable complement to formal learning experiences. One of the biggest challenges with formal learning or training (e.g., a workshop, training program, class) is transfer of learning outside the classroom. In other words, learners may show knowledge acquisition and high levels of engagement in the program, but when they go back to their day-to-day lives or work, keep doing the same things they were doing before.

Imagine this scenario: Rosa attends a training program at work about how to delegate to her employees more effectively. In the four-hour training she is highly interested and engaged with the content. She practices in pair exercises, takes detailed notes, and sets intentions for what she wants to try with her team. Without a coach, Rosa will go back to her regular workday following the training, where she is immediately met with 125 new emails, urgent requests from her manager, 6–7 hours a day of meetings and calls, and a team of 13 direct reports. Not surprisingly, Rosa's intentions for delegating to her team quickly get moved to the back burner, despite her enthusiasm.

In a different version of this story, Rosa is assigned to a peer-coaching group with three other participants from her training program. Before the program ends, they schedule weekly one-hour peer-coaching meetings for the next six weeks. Rosa is adamant about protecting the time on her calendar so she can join each peer-coaching meeting. During the six weekly meetings, she and her teammates practice coaching each other around their intentions for delegating, what they have tried and noticed, what is working and what isn't working. Rosa feels a sense of accountability to act on the intentions she sets, because she wants to have something to share back to the group in their next weekly meeting. The addition of coaching in the weeks following the learning program supports Rosa in achieving her goals of delegating to her team more. The peer-coaching meetings create a sense of accountability and ensure that she has time each week to pause and reflect on what she's trying, what's working, and what she wants to try next. Research has consistently shown that working with a coach after a formal learning program enhances transfer of learning and the likelihood that what was learned in the training will turn into new behaviors outside of the classroom.[26] And, what's most interesting about this finding, is that manager coaching,[27] peer coaching,[28] and working with a professional coach all have a positive impact on transfer of training!

Coaching on its own is also a high-impact tool for leader development. Leaders determine what they want to work on – they set their own goals and identify opportunities to learn by doing – while getting thought partnership, support, structure, and a sense of accountability from working with a coach. Coaching for leader development is high impact because of the tailored, personalized, 1:1 nature. Working with a coach has been linked to myriad important outcomes in leaders' growth, such as increased emotional and social competence,[29] better people management skills, improved communication skills, higher levels of engagement and productivity,[30] greater self-awareness,[31] improved relationships[32] in all directions (up, down, sideways), improved ability to manage and navigate change, higher self-efficacy, greater resilience,[33] and even positive spillover outside of work to family life. This list is far from exhaustive but gives a sense of the many aspects of leader beliefs, behaviors, and capabilities that coaching can target.

Career development

Similar to leader development, coaching can be a powerful tool to support individual career development. Career development is the process of truly owning one's career by investing in new skills, exploring opportunities for growth and/or advancement along a career path, and making deliberate choices about how that career path unfolds. Coaching for career development can take a few different forms. For an individual looking for opportunities to grow and advance within their current role or organization, coaching from a manager, peer, or HR colleague can help them not only pause to reflect on their aspirations, but also support them in acquiring and sharpening new skills and capabilities that are aligned with their aspirations. Organizations that espouse a "grow from within" approach to talent (e.g., hiring people early in their careers and growing them to advance to higher levels of leadership) benefit from having a strong coaching culture where individuals receive the support and thought partnership they need to grow on the job and explore opportunities to advance within that organization. More and more, organizations are looking for ways to deliberately support employees in exploring options for their career path within the organization, and coaching plays an important role in that process.[34] Some organizations even offer career coaching internally; the assumption here is that employees want to grow their career and develop as people and professionals. If organizations want to retain good talent, they must provide opportunities for them to do so. Other organizations have developed programs to support employee career growth and transitions during key moments, such as returning from parental leave. One study found that offering "maternity coaching" to female attorneys returning from parental leave supported them emotionally, practically (navigating the return to work and balancing with parental demands), and in thinking about their longer-term career aspirations.[35]

And of course, there are times when people want to make more pronounced shifts in their careers – such as changing organizations, functions, industries or even exploring a new career entirely. For these bigger shifts, professional career coaches can offer a level of support, partnership, and objectivity that enable career-explorers to figure out what they want in the next step of their careers, what options exist for them, and how to realistically pursue a transition. Career coaches may at times divert from the "purist" coaching approach of being non-directive, to share advice or ideas.[36] But ultimately, it's up to the client what they choose to do with that guidance and advice. In their work on coaching and career development, authors Polly Parker and Michael Arthur[37] note that coaches can help individuals navigate the "three ways of knowing" in intelligent career design: WHY we work (values, motivations, needs), HOW we work (our skills, expertise, what we have to offer), and with WHOM we work (relationships inside and outside of the job). A coach can use their skills of asking helpful questions and listening deeply to support their client in uncovering the answers to these three questions as they explore the next horizon of their career.

Outplacement

Sometimes that next career horizon comes unexpectedly. Coaching can be an invaluable resource during another pivotal moment in one's career: When they are unexpectedly downsized or let go from their organization. Outplacement coaching is a specific form of career coaching that supports individuals in coping with and managing through the change of being let go from their organization, while also thinking through what they want to do next. This type of coaching balances emotional support (helping the client process their experience, creating trust and psychological safety, creating space for reflection and sensemaking) with support on exploring options and aspirations, setting goals, and pursuing a path forward to their next opportunity.

Research has shown that outplacement coaching is particularly productive for a certain profile of individuals. Researchers Harry Martin and Dennis Lekan[38] found that individuals who are higher on three "Big Five" personality trains – openness, agreeableness, and conscientiousness – are more likely to embrace the benefits of outplacement coaching. For instance, they found that individuals high in the trait of openness are more likely to advance in their new roles, and those who are high in agreeableness and conscientiousness are more likely to feel satisfied and perform at a high level in their new roles, post outplacement. They also found that highly agreeable individuals show more resilience and coping in response to the outplacement experience. These results don't suggest that individuals low on these traits will not benefit from outplacement coaching, but they do reinforce the power of the personalized nature of coaching. An outplacement coach who understands where a client stands on these dimensions can tailor their approach accordingly to best support the client – meeting them where they are.

Offering outplacement coaching is also beneficial to the organization. Making downsizing decisions and letting employees go is stressful and filled with uncertainty. Being able to offer a service that truly supports those individuals in navigating the next phase of their career can make these changes feel more caring and people-centric, and increase the likelihood that individuals leave with a positive attitude toward the organization.

In this chapter we have explored a variety of ways that coaching can be applied within organizations. Coaching can be provided by managers, peers, or HR professionals who have a robust coaching skill set. Professional coaches can provide more high-touch and structured support when objectivity, capacity, accountability, and a more advanced skill set are needed. A coaching approach can be used to modernize performance management processes and support development and growth, not just evaluation. And coaching can take other people practices (learning, leader development, career development, outplacement) to a higher level of impact. We explored the impact of coaching on organizational culture, and what it takes to intentionally develop a culture for coaching within an organization. We focused on the benefits of coaching for individuals within those organizations and for the organization as a whole. Whether it's through formal mechanisms like hiring professional coaches to serve in internal or external coaching roles, or informally through peer coaching, building a coaching culture, or building systems to be enabling rather than coercive, coaching can have a positive impact on organizations. Organizations are fundamentally powered by people, and people have an innate desire to be seen, be heard, and feel that their opinions and perspectives matter.

In the next and final chapter, we examine the impact coaching can have outside of our professional lives. A coaching mindset can shift your understanding of and ability to navigate the world around you. We will weave together concepts from these first six chapters and share ideas for how you can bring your coaching mindset and skill set to relationships and situations in all parts of your life.

Chapter 6 Key idea

Coaching can be incorporated in organizations in formal and informal ways to impact individuals, groups, teams, and culture. Viewing organizational practices and processes can impact how they are designed and implemented.

Want to learn more? Check out

The Institute of Coaching (IOC) offers an introduction to organizational coaching. Check out their website: https://instituteofcoaching.org/resources/introduction-organizational-coaching

Curious about coach training programs? Check out the full list of programs on the International Coaching Federation's Website:

https://coachingfederation.org/coaching-education

Recommended reading

Executive coaching: a guide for the HR professional by Anna Marie Valerio and Robert J. *Lee*

Measuring the success of coaching by Patti Phillips, Jack Phillips, and Lisa Edwards

Reinventing organizations: a guide to creating organizations inspired by the next stage in human consciousness by Frederic Laloux

Transforming performance management to drive performance: an evidence-based roadmap by Rose A. Mueller-Hanson and Elaine Pulakos

Notes

1 Schein, E. H. (2004). *Organisational culture and leadership* (3rd ed.). San Francisco, CA: Jossey Bass.
2 Schneider, B. (2021). People management in work organizations: Fifty years of learnings. *Organizational Dynamics*, 50(4), 6, 100789. https://doi.org/10.1016/j.orgdyn.2020.100789
3 Bennett, J. L., & Bush, M. W. (2011). High-Impact Coaching for Organizational Change. *International Journal of Coaching in Organisations*, 8(32), 114–123.
4 Grant, A. M., Curtayne, L., & Burton, G. (2009). Executive coaching enhances goal attainment, resilience and workplace well-being: A randomised controlled study. *The Journal of Positive Psychology, 4*(5), 396–407. https://doi.org/10.1080/17439760902992456
  Sherlock-Storey, M., Moss, M., & Timson, S. (2013). Brief coaching for resilience during organisational change – An exploratory study. *The Coaching Psychologist, 9*(1), 19–26.
  Timson, S. (2015). Exploring what clients find helpful in a brief resilience coaching programme: A qualitative study. *The Coaching Psychologist, 11*(2), 81–88.
5 Eatough, E. (2021, November 17). Managers have a strong effect on team performance, for better or worse. *BetterUp*. www.betterup.com/blog/managers-strong-effect-on-team-performance
6 International Coaching Federation. (2020). *ICF global coaching study*. https://coachfederation.org/app/uploads/2020/09/FINAL_ICF_GCS2020_Executive Summary.pdf

7 Peterson, D. B. (2010). Executive coaching: A critical review and recommendations for advancing the practice. In S. Zedeck (Ed.), *APA handbook of industrial and organizational psychology: Vol. 2. Selecting and developing members of the organization* (pp. 527–566). Washington, DC: American Psychological Association. https://doi.org/10.1037/12170-018

8 Stover, J. (2016, March 11). Stages of maturity for organizational coaching practices. *LinkedIn*. www.linkedin.com/pulse/stages-maturity-organizational-coaching-practices-jeremy-stover-pcc/

9 Robichaux, A. (2021, October 8). Building the human transformation company: The principles that shape our future. *BetterUp*. www.betterup.com/blog/human-transformation-company-principles

10 Persley, N., Baughman, W. A., Morath, R., Holt, R., & Maher, M. A. (1994, July). *Defining developmental environments: Curriculum design strategies promoting positive reactions to demanding courses* [Conference Presentation]. APS 1994 Convention, Washington, DC.

11 Schneider. (2021). People management, 6, 100789.

12 De Vries, M. K. (2008). *Leadership coaching and organizational transformation: Effectiveness in a world of paradoxes*. Fontainebleau: INSEAD Working Papers Series. https://flora.insead.edu/fichiersti_wp/inseadwp2008/2008-71.pdf

13 Laloux, F. (2014). *Reinventing organizations: A guide to creating organizations inspired by the next stage of human consciousness*. Brussels: Nelson Parker.

14 Kegan, R., & Lahey, L. L. (2016). *An everyone culture: Becoming a deliberately developmental organization*. Boston, MA: Harvard Business Review Press.

15 Kaufman, S. B. (2021). *Transcend: The new science of self-actualization*. New York: Penguin Random House.

16 Kurtessis, J. N., Eisenberger, R., Ford, M. T., Buffardi, L. C., Stewart, K. A., & Adis, C. S. (2017). Perceived organizational support: A meta-analytic evaluation of organizational support theory. *Journal of Management, 43*(6), 1854–1884. https://doi.org/10.1177/0149206315575554

   Aguinis, H., & Kraiger, K. (2009). Benefits of training and development for individuals and teams, organizations, and society. *Annual Review of Psychology, 60*(1), 451–474. https://doi.org/10.1146/annurev.psych.60.110707.163505

17 Kegan & Lahey. (2016). *An everyone culture.*

18 Schein, E. H. (2016). *Humble consulting: How to provide real help faster*. Oakland CA: Berrett-Koehler Publishers.

19 Arias, M. E., Riordan, B. G., & Thom, A. (2018). Developing an organizational coaching strategy and culture. In N. van Dam (Ed.), *Elevating learning and development: Insights and practical guidance from the field* (pp. 224–235). New York, NY: McKinsey & Company.

20 Schneider, B., González-Romá, V., Ostroff, C., & West, M. A. (2017). Organizational climate and culture: Reflections on the history of the constructs in the Journal of Applied Psychology. *Journal of Applied Psychology, 102*(3), 468–482. https://doi.org/10.1037/apl0000090

21 Cardinal, L. B., Kreutzer, M., & Miller, C. C. (2017). An aspirational view of organizational control research: Re-invigorating empirical work to better meet

the challenges of 21st century organizations. *Academy of Management Annals, 11*(2), 559–592. https://doi.org/10.5465/annals.2014.0086

22 Colquitt, A., & Goldberg, E. (In Press). Flipping the script on performance management: from evaluation to enablement. In R Silzer, B. R. Scott, & W. C. Borman (Eds.), *Handbook on the practice of industrial/organizational psychology: Leveraging psychology for individual and organizational effectiveness.* Oxford, UK: Oxford University Press.

23 Carenys, J. (2012). Management control systems: A historical perspective. *International Journal of Economy, Management and Social Sciences, 1*(1), 1–18.

24 Smither, J. W., London, M., Flautt, R., Vargas, Y., & Kucine, I. (2003). Can working with an executive coach improve multisource feedback ratings over time? A quasi-experimental field study. *Personnel Psychology, 56*(1), 23–44. https://doi.org/10.1111/j.1744-6570.2003.tb00142.x

25 Luthans, F., & Peterson, S. J. (2003). 360-degree feedback with systematic coaching: Empirical analysis suggests a winning combination. *Human Resource Management, 42*(3), 243–256. https://doi.org/10.1002/hrm.10083

26 Spencer, L. (2011). Coaching and training transfer: A phenomenological inquiry into combined training-coaching programmes. *International Journal of Evidence Based Coaching & Mentoring, 5,* 1–18.
   Olivero, G., Bane, K. D., & Kopelman, R. E. (1997). Executive coaching as a transfer of training tool: Effects on productivity in a public agency. *Public Personnel Management, 26*(4), 461–469. https://doi.org/10.1177/009102609702600403

27 Hagen, M. S. (2012). Managerial coaching: A review of the literature. *Performance Improvement Quarterly, 24*(4), 17–39. https://doi.org/10.1002/piq.20123

28 Showers, B. (1984). *Peer coaching: A strategy for facilitating transfer of training. A CEPM R&D report.* Oregon University Eugene. Center for Educational Policy and Management. https://eric.ed.gov/?id=ed271849

29 Van Oosten, E. B., McBride-Walker, S. M., & Taylor, S. N. (2019). Investing in what matters: The impact of emotional and social competency development and executive coaching on leader outcomes. *Consulting Psychology Journal: Practice and Research, 71*(4), 249–269. https://doi.org/10.1037/cpb0000141

30 Kombarakaran, F. A., Yang, J. A., Baker, M. N., & Fernandes, P. B. (2008). Executive coaching: It works! *Consulting Psychology Journal: Practice and Research, 60*(1), 78–90. https://doi.org/10.1037/1065-9293.60.1.78

31 Sutton, A., & Crobach, C. (2022). Improving self-awareness and engagement through group coaching. *International Journal of Evidence Based Coaching & Mentoring, 20*(1), 35–49.

32 McGovern, J., Lindemann, M., Vergara, M., Murphy, S., Barker, L., & Warrenfeltz, R. (2001). Maximizing the impact of executive coaching. *The Manchester Review, 6*(1), 1–9.

33 Grant, A. M. (2014). The efficacy of executive coaching in times of organisational change. *Journal of Change Management, 14*(2), 258–280. https://doi.org/10.1080/14697017.2013.805159

34 Frigerio, G., & Rix, S. (2021). Career development and coaching: Straddling two worlds and bringing them together. *Journal of the National Institute for Career Education and Counselling, 46*(1), 32–38. https://doi.org/10.20856/jnicec.4606

35 Filsinger, C. (2012). How can maternity coaching influence women's re-engagement with their career development: A case study of a maternity coaching programme in UK-based private law firms. *International Journal of Evidence Based Coaching & Mentoring, 6*, 46–56.

36 Frigerio & Rix. (2021). Career development and coaching, 32–38.

37 Parker, P., & Arthur, M. B. (2004). Coaching for career development and leadership development: An intelligent career approach. *Australian Journal of Career Development, 13*(3), 55–60. https://doi.org/10.1177/103841620401300311

38 Martin, H. J., & Lekan, D. F. (2008). Individual differences in outplacement success. *Career Development International, 13*(5), 425–439. https://doi.org/10.1108/13620430810891455

7
Taking your coaching approach out into the world

Questions we'll answer in this chapter:

1. How can coaching skills be applied outside of work?
2. How can a coaching mindset be applied to societal challenges?
3. What should I be aware of as I start to incorporate coaching in my day-to-day life?

Eva is at her wit's end. Her son, A.J., is three years old and in the stage that his family lovingly refers to as a "three-nager." He wants what he wants, when he wants it, and when he doesn't get it, he screams, cries, and lashes out; he can even get violent. During these episodes, Eva tries her best to stay calm, but she has a lot going on. She has a never-ending to-do list running through her mind that spans her roles at work, at home, and in her community. Her own needs often don't even make the list. In fact, some days she forgets to eat, and it has gotten to the point where a shower feels like a luxury. She's trying to respond to emails and get her work done when A.J. walks in to ask her to open a snack for him. She stops mid-sentence in the email she's writing and sees that he's holding candy. When she tells him he can't have it, he begins to scream and throw himself on the ground. He starts kicking his arms and legs. Eva immediately feels her heart rate go up and her cheeks get flushed. She begins by trying to shush him so she can talk to him about her reasoning and find something else for him. None of that works, and she notices that she now has just two minutes before her next meeting. She loses her patience and snaps at him: "A.J., I don't have time for this! You can't have candy before dinner! Can't you see that Mommy is busy? Now go sit in time out until you calm down!"

It felt effective at the time. Eva moved A.J. to his room, which helped with the noise. She knew that he was safe and that allowing him to eat sugar was not going to do either of them any favors. Yet, the interaction nagged at her for the rest of the day. She worried that her reaction made it seem like he wasn't as important as the meeting. She kept picturing him alone in his room, still hungry. She started to wonder whether the tantrum was about not getting the candy when he wanted it or about not getting her attention when he wanted it. She went into a bit of a spiral, feeling guilty about not being more patient with him and comparing herself to the other moms she knew. Part of her knew it was silly, but it gnawed at her because it was neither how she wanted to show up nor congruent with her vision of herself as a parent.

In this book, we've introduced you to coaching mindsets and skills and to how adopting them can powerfully impact you and your interactions with others. We've covered how this shows up in interactions with individuals (1:1), in groups or teams, and in organizations. We spend a lot of our time in those contexts, but we play many roles outside of "employee." There's a world outside of organizations that we exist in and that in turn impacts our world at work. In this chapter we turn our focus outside of organizations. We start with ways in which coaching can impact the most meaningful roles you play outside of work – parent, child, spouse, neighbor, and so on. We tackle how your coaching skills can be used to shift how you show up in those roles to better navigate conflict and build connection. Looking even more expansively, we examine how a coaching mindset can shift the way you look at the world and how it might be relevant to pervasive global challenges such as racism, sexism, political polarization, climate change, and beyond. We end by reiterating how the things within your control – your ability to be present, curious, open, and non-judgmental – can be used to create a better world.

The many hats we wear

Most people will spend about a third of their lives at work. Work plays an important role in providing financial security, social interaction, and can be a source of meaning and purpose. This often leads us to think first about how we might apply coaching skills to the roles we play at work – employee, colleague, leader, mentor, and so on. And yet, how we show up in one place tends to be how we show up everywhere. Our ability to become more curious, open, and non-judgmental (CON) is likely to spill over into the many roles you play outside of work as well. As with any change, it's even more likely if you set an intention around it.

When Shonna went through coach training, she did so with two primary goals: (1) to expand her organizational effectiveness toolkit by better equipping herself to help leaders grow and develop and (2) to use the tools on herself to set better boundaries at work and tackle her chronic workaholism. What she started noticing, however, was that she couldn't turn it off. She started seeing opportunities in her marriage to communicate more clearly and listen more deeply. She had two young children at the time and started seeing her role as a parent not as shaping them, but instead to help them discover their own shape. She noticed she was asking her friends different kinds of questions and was better able to see alternative perspectives – even if she felt a lot of conviction about a topic. The impact on each of those roles was unexpected and positive. What was it that led to such a broad and diverse impact?

In this book we have taken a close look at what it means to adopt a coaching mindset and develop your coaching skill set. We explored processes in your brain that influence how you perceive your experiences and the world around you, which ultimately impacts your behavior. We've emphasized the value of being a new kind of "CON artist" (practicing curiosity, openness and non-judgment). We've seen how key coaching skills of listening, asking questions, and noticing can benefit you and others in both 1:1 and group settings. The foundational belief underlying coaching is that people are creative, resourceful, and whole. Because they are creative, resourceful, and whole, we don't have to fix them. We don't need to solve their problems because they can solve them on their own. We don't have the answers for them because they are the experts in their own lives. This fuels our curiosity because this means that their choices and beliefs are the natural outcomes of who they are and their lived experiences. To be in service to them, we have the opportunity to help them gain greater clarity into what they want, challenge them to see things in multiple ways, and enable them to tap into their own wisdom. Doing so requires that we develop our curiosity and openness, practice non-judgment, and develop our skills in listening.

Michael Bungay Stanier, author of some of our favorite coaching books, like *The Coaching Habit*[1] and *The Advice Trap*,[2] has a practice of making himself a list of how he wants to show up on a card that he keeps in his pocket. He refers to it as "This, Not That." We love this as a simple way to remind yourself of what it looks like when you are at your best (in this case showing up a little more coach-like) or not.

This | Not That

This	Not That
Adopt a CON mindset (curious, open, non-judgemental)	Let your biases and assumptions color your perceptions
Believe the other person is creative, resourceful, and whole and can solve their own problems	Believe that you are right and need to offer direction or advice
Listen with your ears and full attention	Engage in lazy listening or try to multitask
Listen to understand	Listen to respond or judge
Ask open-ended questions (e.g., what, how)	Ask questions that can be answered with yes or no or that prompt defensiveness
Ask simple, single questions	Wrap your questions in preamble or post-amble
Let the other person finish speaking	Assume you know what they are thinking or try to finish their sentences for them
Hold up the mirror and share what you notice about the other person's behavior	Make assumptions about what people want or why they are doing something
Embrace silence	Fill the space
Hold space for others' experience	Take on others' experience

 Experience it yourself

What roles do you play? Use this reflection exercise to explore.

Take 2 minutes to quickly list every role you play in your life as they come to mind.

_____

_____

_____

Go back through the list. Did you write them in order of importance? Reflect on what roles feel most central to your identity. Reorder them if you need to.

_____

_____

_____

In what role would you like to shift how you show up? How might adopting a coaching mindset or skill set help?

_____

_____

_____

What's one small experiment you want to commit to trying?

_____

_____

_____

Looking for an opening

In his book *Coaching: Evoking Excellence in Others*,[3] professional coach and author James Flaherty notes that all coaching begins with an opening. We've alluded to openings a few times in earlier chapters. An opening may look like a need or request for support, a change from routine, a moment of crisis or struggle, an opportunity to notice or share an observation. According to Flaherty, all coaching begins with an opening. An opening could look like a friend saying, "I'm really torn about what to do in this situation," your teenage child saying, "Ugh! No one understands!" or sharing implications of an upcoming organizational change with a member of your team. Whatever the topic or situation, the door cracks open for you to practice your skills of noticing, really listening, or asking a question in service to that person. In Eva's case, A.J.'s tantrum presented an opening, if she was willing to see it and take it. In that moment, Eva could have paused for just a moment to notice what was happening, to think about how she wanted to respond, rather than react, and make a conscious choice about how to engage with A.J. to understand what he really wanted and how she could balance that with her work. The ability to notice an opening, however, depends on the focus of your attention. Eva's attention was divided in the moment; she was mostly focused on the work she was trying to complete and only partially on what was going on with A.J. Let's take a look at the importance of mindfulness and being fully present in order to notice openings and choose to use our coaching capabilities.

Mindfulness and presence

In our class on coaching skills at Georgetown University, our students begin the semester by committing to a mindfulness practice. Each week, we expose them to a new tool for practicing mindfulness. In those early weeks, we suspect that some of the students wonder what we are doing and why. Why are mindful eating, a mindful walk, mindfully listening to music, and paying attention to our breathing relevant to coaching? Once we get to the midpoint of the semester, we always seem to get a few unsolicited comments from students about how practicing mindfulness has helped them be more present and focused in their conversations with others, and also feel calmer and less overwhelmed in their work and personal lives. They begin to look forward to it and some even start to bring the practice into their personal and work lives.

Practicing mindfulness enables us to be fully present in the current moment, which means giving whatever is in front of us our full attention and awareness. This may sound reminiscent of our take on *really* listening, and that's because to really listen we must be fully present in that moment, with that person. Distractions from our environment, cell phones, and inner monologue all pull us away from being fully present and in the moment. Practicing mindfulness is like strengthening the muscle that allows us to be fully present. It means focusing completely on what we are experiencing in the moment, without judgment or interpretation.

Professor, coach, and author Jonathan Passmore has done extensive work on the role of mindfulness in coaching. He articulates four ways that mindfulness enhances coaching: preparing for coaching, maintaining focus on the session, remaining emotionally detached, and teaching mindfulness to the person we are coaching.[4] Pausing for a mindful moment before entering a coaching conversation allows us to leave behind whatever we were doing before the conversation and be fully present and focused. This could include sitting with our feet flat on the floor and taking four deep breaths to get centered and present in the moment. Practicing mindfulness throughout the conversation ensures that our attention stays with the other person and doesn't wander off to places that are NOT here – such as what to have for dinner, what you need to do to prepare for your meeting this afternoon or wondering why it's so cold in this room.

Now, on that last point: distractions can arise despite your very best efforts. Remember back in Chapter 4 where we mentioned the possibility of construction noise negatively impacting your ability to listen? Once, Brodie was on a Zoom call with a coaching client when the building across the street from her home literally caught on fire. Brodie did her best to ignore the black smoke and flames shooting out the windows (this is not an exaggeration). She said nothing about it to her client and did her best to stay focused on the conversation. But there is no doubt that a substantial portion of Brodie's attention was pulled away – because of curiosity, fear, or concern for the people inside the building. It's likely that her client picked up on a shift in Brodie's attention. As we mentioned in Chapter 4, in a situation like this, you may be best served to use your skill of *naming* to acknowledge the distraction and figure out the best way to manage it. In Brodie's case, she could have said, "I'm so sorry to do this, but can we take a five-minute break? The building across the street from me is on fire, and I just need to make sure everything is okay over here." Surely Brodie's client would have completely understood. By naming what is going on and taking a deliberate pause, Brodie would have ensured that her client didn't attribute Brodie's wandering attention to her or the conversation – she would have known that the distraction was external and unrelated to the conversation.

Once that (literal) fire has been put out and we can refocus on the conversation, Passmore notes that practicing mindfulness can also help us remain emotionally detached during a conversation. In Chapter 2, we mentioned that we are all living our own "story" in which we are both the hero and the narrator. When using your coaching skills, remaining emotionally detached ensures that you don't also get sucked into the other person's story. Remaining objective is paramount to being in support of the person that you are coaching. There is nothing wrong with experiencing empathy and understanding toward what the other person is experiencing, but once you are pulled into the emotional experience with that person, you are no longer able to stand side-by-side with them and help them work through their own challenges. In coaching, we often refer to this as "holding space" for the other person. If we get sucked into the story, we can't hold the space – we're in it. Mindfulness plays an important role in noticing our emotions without immediately reacting to them. When we are fully present and practicing mindfulness in a coaching conversation, we can empathize and notice the other person's emotions, notice the impact on our own emotions, and choose to remain objective to best serve and support the other person.

Staying present in a world designed to distract you

Our ability to manage distractions and avoid the temptation to multitask is so important for being fully present. Practicing mindfulness can help us strengthen our attention muscles and stay focused on what is happening

Holding Space

in front of us, but for many this requires substantial self-control. We live in a world littered with distractions, and many of us operate in environments where the ability to multitask is highly valued or even expected. For example, Nora works in an organization that relies heavily on an instant messaging app. This app has many wonderful benefits for boosting collaboration and communication, cutting down on email traffic, and sending colleagues funny memes and GIFs. It also allows a flood of notifications and instant messages from colleagues looking for a quick response. Nora's organization has an unspoken norm of keeping this instant messaging app on all the time – on employees' laptops, phones, while they are working on other things, and while they are on conference calls. Fast response time is highly valued in this culture. Every day at work, Nora finds herself spending five to six hours on conference calls or video conferences. Of course, the rest of her work doesn't slow down in the meantime, which means during those hours she finds herself trying to pay attention to the call while also fielding instant messages and requests from colleagues all over the organization (and all over the world). At the end of the day, Nora feels frazzled, overwhelmed, and fatigued. She finds that she often makes small mistakes in her instant messaging responses and can only tell you about 60% of what was discussed on the calls. Nora really dislikes this expectation for constant multitasking. One day at work, the messaging app was down, and she was able to be fully present and focused on her calls. She took so much more away from the conversations, felt like she made meaningful contributions to the discussion, and felt calmer and clearer at the end of the day.

Nora is experiencing the strain of rapidly switching between tasks because, despite what her colleagues believe, humans struggle to do two things at the same time, particularly if the tasks require the same part of your brain to be in charge.[5] In other words, anytime you believe that you are multitasking – say, writing an email and listening to a podcast – your attention is simply moving back and forth from one activity to the other (exception: if one of those behaviors is automatic, like walking). This usually translates to doing both things with mediocrity and compromised attention. Now, why is this relevant to a book about coaching skills? If you intend to be fully present and give a conversation your complete attention, you simply cannot try to do something else at the same time. You certainly cannot practice mindfulness when splitting your attention between two (or more!) things. You cannot really listen to someone *and* sneak a glimpse at that text message that just came in on your phone.

As we mentioned in Chapter 4, it's easy to be a lazy listener – to go through the motions of hearing without really giving the other person your full attention. And it's easy to mistakenly assume that the other person doesn't notice. We asked our students: How can you tell when someone isn't really listening? Here's what they shared:

- "Their eyes are somewhere else – looking down, looking behind you. Even sort of looking 'through' you."
- "They say things like 'yeah, uh-huh, oh, yeah, wow' in a way that sounds bored and disconnected from what you are sharing."
- "They ask a question about something you already addressed."
- "They give you advice or make a comment about something you already covered."
- "They actually say, 'I'm sorry I missed that – can you please say it again.' But at least in that case they admit it!"
- "They have an emotional reaction that is totally out of sync with what you're talking about. Once I was talking about complications with my pregnancy, and the other person laughed and made some generic comment. It was really weird."
- "You can hear them doing something else. Once I was on a call with my boss talking about a serious challenge I was facing and I could hear him typing in the background."

You may recognize some of these tells. You might even recognize some of them in yourself. In other words, despite our best efforts at faking real listening, other people easily pick up on verbal and physical cues that we aren't really listening. Think about your own experience for a moment.

Experience it yourself

Recall a time when you were speaking to someone and you could tell they weren't really listening. What did you notice about their behavior?

_____

_____

_____

What did it feel like when you realized that person wasn't really listening to you?

_____

_____

_____

When others go through the motions of listening, this can have a strong negative impact on the person who is speaking. Their emotional reactions could range from disappointment, to anger, to feeling small or unimportant. Depending on the relationship, not really listening can erode trust and the strength of the relationship. It sends a message to the speaker that what they have to say isn't important or interesting. They may even internalize this and come to believe that THEY are not important, interesting, or deserving of your attention. Really listening and giving others our full attention is important in any interaction if we care about that person and our relationship with them. It's also critically important in a coaching conversation, where we aspire to create space for the other person to be open and vulnerable.

Using curiosity to reel in your wandering mind

Like the band the Human League said in their 1986 classic song, we're all "only human,"[6] which means that sometimes we struggle to bring our best listening skills or our full attention to a conversation. Sometimes the conversation is simply boring. Sometimes we have other pressing matters on our minds that creep in despite our best efforts to be mindful and present. Sometimes we are sleep deprived and paying attention is physically challenging! In these moments, our curiosity can once again be a powerful tool. Turning on your curiosity can help you stay present, interested, and engaged in the

Experience it yourself

What are the greatest threats to your ability to be fully present (e.g., your phone, your work environment, your proclivity for shiny objects)?

_____

_____

_____

What will you try to better manage that threat next time you want to be fully present in a conversation?

_____

_____

_____

How do you like to practice mindfulness? Or, what do you want to try?

_____

_____

_____

conversation. Research has shown that getting curious about others increases the quality of our listening and helps us to put ourselves in their shoes,[7] which is an essential part of practicing empathy. Curiosity also boosts engagement and interest in what we are paying attention to. Research has shown that humans can have both a "trait" and "state" level of curiosity,[8] meaning that some people are more naturally curious than others (trait), and that we can all make choices to intentionally "turn on" and practice our curiosity (state).

In addition to helping us be more present and engaged with others, curiosity also unlocks myriad other positive behaviors that contribute to individual and organizational performance. Zander Lurie, CEO of SurveyMonkey, found that curiosity was the most prevalent attribute among their highest performing employees AND their best customers.[9] Research has also shown that curiosity leads to more creativity and innovation in solving problems, more adaptive responses to stress (less defensiveness, reactivity, and aggression), more information sharing, and higher job performance.[10] In May 2021, a school bus in South Carolina was the target of an armed hijack. In addition to the bus driver, 18 kindergartners were on the bus during the hijacking. What happened next demonstrates the power of genuine curiosity, which comes naturally to six-year-olds. The kindergartners started peppering the hijacker with curious questions:[11]

"Why are you doing this?"
"Are you a soldier?"
"Are you going to hurt us?"
"Are you going to hurt our bus driver?"

After enough kindergarten interrogation, the hijacker asked the driver to stop the bus, and he ran off. The bus driver attributes the safe outcome of the situation to the kids' natural curiosity. In this case, the curious questions must have been too much for the hijacker to handle. Let this also be a reminder to self-manage as you express your curiosity – remember to ask one question at a time so you don't overwhelm your companion.

Another way to boost curiosity and engagement in a conversation is to choose what we are listening for. For example, you can choose to listen for emotion and pay very close attention to the feelings and emotions that the other person is conveying. You might set an intention to learn what really matters to that person – when do they "light up," lean in, and start speaking at a quicker pace? You could get even more specific and choose to listen intently for positive emotions. You could make a point of really watching for and noticing facial expressions. You could listen with the intent of noticing their biases, assumptions, their "story," and lens of perception. Choosing to listen for something specific can boost engagement and presence by further directing our attention.

Taking your coaching skills out into the world

Let's turn back to Eva. There wasn't anything egregious about how she responded to A.J. in her story. It's a scene most parents (or aunts, uncles, cousins, teachers) can relate to. But we can start to imagine that Eva doesn't like the feeling she has when she loses her patience with A.J. She might accept that she won't achieve perfection, but she wants to practice responding differently in those inevitable moments of frustration. Imagine that, like Shonna, Eva learned more about coaching. She started a mindfulness practice. This gave her the tools she needed to notice when she was feeling stressed or irritated and pause before responding. She had experienced what it felt like to be truly seen and heard and wanted to recreate that feeling for A.J. as often as she could. She recognized his outburst as being "hijacked."

She got down to his eye level and spoke calmly and gave A.J. choices about what he could have instead. She was also able to name when *she* got hijacked and take a few deep breaths. She tested her hypothesis that he might just want her attention and sent a note to her colleagues that she'd be a few minutes late to her meeting. This gave her the time she needed to connect with A.J. and explain when she'd be finished and what they would do together. These small changes might add up to something meaningful over time. They might help her support A.J. in feeling secure, developing better emotional regulation skills, and equip him to navigate his needs and choices.

You can use your coaching mindset and skills to positively impact situations across the many roles you play in your work and life. Imagine this: You are attending Thanksgiving dinner with your family, who are visiting from all over the United States. Somehow, inevitably, the conversation turns to the Presidential election. Your uncle, whom you see once or twice per year, has very strong political views that seem to be the opposite of your own. Your uncle talks about everything that is wrong in America, making sweeping statements about various populations of people, industries, political parties and more. Perhaps you feel tempted to jump in and counter all his complaints and point out his flawed thinking, not to mention everything that's wrong about his preferred party. Where do you think that will take the conversation? Probably into an unpleasant spiral of disagreement, broad generalizations, listening to respond, and angst and discomfort for everyone else at the table. It may devolve into a verbal ping-pong match where neither you nor your uncle are listening – you're too busy coming up with the smart thing you will say next to "be right" in this debate. Your inner monologue might include thoughts like, "What an idiot," "I can't believe I'm related to this man," or "He is everything that is wrong with America."

What if, instead, you brought your coaching skills to the conversation? You approach your uncle and his statements with a mindset of curiosity, openness, and non-judgment. You allow yourself to get curious about what in his lived experience enables him to see something you don't see. Rather than listening to respond and poke holes in his statements, you listen to understand where he is coming from. You become aware of his ladder of inference. You become aware of your own ladder of inference. You ask questions to draw him out, rather than responding with strong statements and disagreement. Perhaps you will discover that what your uncle is really struggling with is feeling left behind or irrelevant as the world around him changes rapidly, at a pace he can't keep up with. You may get to the heart of what he really cares about and what's important to him and discover that you have shared values of hard work, recognition, and caring for your family. Though you may not end the conversation agreeing on anything related to politics, you will end the conversation knowing more about him and strengthening, rather than eroding, your relationship. You might leave seeing more of his humanity, rather than confirming a caricature you had in your mind of people who share his perspective.

Your coaching skills can also be a powerful tool for influence or negotiation. Our attempts at both tactics are easily derailed by assumptions we make about other people or situations. Using your coaching skills of asking questions and really listening can help you surface what others really care about – which may be wildly different from what you assumed. Take Harold, for example. Harold is planning a vacation for himself and his partner, Cheryl. Harold wants a beach vacation and is really excited about an all-inclusive resort he found. His typical approach has been "selling" the idea to Cheryl. He considers himself to be pretty convincing but is disappointed when Cheryl shares that she's just not excited about it.

Now let's pretend that Harold takes a class or reads a book about coaching skills. He decides to experiment with using those skills to navigate the negotiation on where to vacation with Cheryl. Rather than holding onto resentment or trying to convince Cheryl to go with his idea, he approaches the next conversation from a place of curiosity and openness, not trying to "sell her" on his idea. He asks open-ended questions and listens closely to what's important to her about the vacation and what she wants to get out of it rather than focusing on what he will say next to convince her that this option is the best one. He discovers that Cheryl has been feeling restless and is looking for inspiration and adventure rather than relaxation. He remembers seeing another resort that offered both – a nice beach setting but with a wide range of excursions in a country and culture that neither of them had prior exposure to. Had he not asked questions and gotten curious about her interests, he would have focused on selling her the initial vacation idea and missed the opportunity to meet both of their needs. By weaving his coaching skills into his approach to their decision, Harold gets to know more about Cheryl, strengthen their relationship, and make connections between their respective needs and the choices available to them.

Understanding what other people care about is paramount to influencing their decision making or coming to an agreement in negotiation. Former hostage negotiator Chris Voss,[12] describes negotiation tips that seem eerily familiar to coaching skills – asking questions to build empathy, labeling, mirroring, asking "what" and "how" questions, and using silence. Getting curious, asking questions, and really listening can lead to recommendations and solutions that align with that person's interests, goals, and preferences. For example, understanding that a benefit of eldercare is more important to a new hire than more vacation time will lead to a more productive and satisfying compensation negotiation. A sommelier who asks a restaurant patron about their wine preferences and desired price point will make a better recommendation than a sommelier who is focused on selling a particular bottle of wine that night. A car dealer who asks questions to learn that a car-buyer cares about gas mileage and safety will have greater luck closing the deal than the salesperson who tries to push his favorite model (or the model that they need to move off the lot). Once more, these are not pure coaching conversations – they are an application of your coaching skills to situations that come up in work and life every day.

Boundaries and ethics in your practice

While we believe that your coaching skills can serve you every day in a variety of settings and interactions, one important caveat that we want to offer is respecting others' boundaries when practicing your coaching skills. Your ability to be curious, open, and non-judgmental will benefit you and whomever you are interacting with. Truly listening with your ears and full attention will help you better understand a person or situation and ensure that others feel heard and understood. Asking open-ended questions is such an important way to overcome your own assumptions and biases, to practice your curiosity out loud, to support others in thinking through problems and potential solutions, and for you to learn more about others and the world around you. We also believe that these skills work beautifully in conjunction with your other wide array of communication skills, like sharing feedback, declaring, making requests, or asserting.

Our hope is that you take from this book all the ways that you can flexibly use these skills. Using your coaching skills does not mean you have to go around having in-depth coaching conversations with everyone, all the time. In fact, we believe that going into full-fledged coaching mode without others' permission can feel intrusive, something we refer to as "guerilla coaching." Is that really what they want and need at that moment? As professional coaches, we can recognize when our other coach friends and colleagues slip into coaching mode with us, and it can feel uncomfortable and at times even unhelpful. Instead, start by thinking about what the agreement is or explicitly ask what the person needs or expects from you in each interaction. In fact, early in our relationship Shonna noticed that Brodie was consistently showing up in a "coach-like" posture. Although Shonna enjoyed and benefited a lot from their interactions, she didn't want Brodie to feel like she was "on." She wanted Brodie to have equal space to have an opinion, a perspective, or to assert something. By initiating a coaching conversation without an agreement with the other person you may be crossing a boundary that you don't yet have permission to cross or shifting the nature of the relationship in a way the other person isn't excited about.

There is a fine line here between exercising your coaching skills (noticing, listening, asking a curious question) and jumping into a full-blown coaching conversation. There are a few ways that you can manage a situation where you think coaching might be of service to the other person. First, you can try what we like to call, "dipping a toe": you practice your listening and then try noticing or asking a curious question. See how it lands with the other person. Where does the conversation go next? Do they seem interested and engaged in having a coaching conversation? Second, you can try making an offer (remember offers from speech acts in Chapter 4?). This might sound like, "Ali, would it be helpful to have a coaching conversation about this?" Third, and our favorite, is asking the other person what they need right now. This might sound like, "Ali, you sound frustrated. How can I best support you?" You can also offer a few forms of support, such as, "What would be most helpful right now? You could vent, I can just listen, or I can be a thought partner." This is our preferred approach to talking with friends and family members. We offer several ways that we can be present for them and allow them to choose and indicate what they are looking for in this moment.

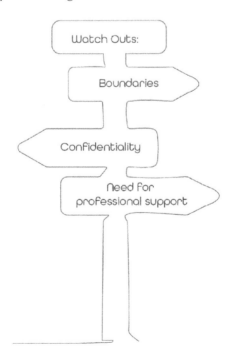

In addition to respecting others' boundaries, a few other ethical consider-ations can arise in your coaching conversations. Research has shown that trust is one of the most important predictors of a successful, effective coach-ing relationship.[13] When trust is present in the conversation, the person being coached feels more comfortable being open, honest, and vulnerable. This level of candor can lead to an unfiltered, unconstrained conversation that allows the client to fully explore the situation, their experience, their feelings, motivations, and what they really want. As a result, confidential-ity is of the utmost importance. Perhaps you've heard that slogan, "What happens in Vegas stays in Vegas." Well, what happens in a coaching conver-sation stays in a coaching conversation. One of the fastest ways for a coach to erode trust and damage a relationship is to share pieces of the coaching conversation outside of the conversation – either with others, or in contexts that feel like a boundary violation. For example, pretend like you are the president of the parent/teacher organization (PTO) at your child's school. You use your coaching skills to help the PTO treasurer think through a chal-lenging situation. The conversation goes great, and the treasurer walks away with new insights and a solution. Later that week, you and the PTO treas-urer are at a neighborhood block party. Beers in hand, you casually mention some specifics from the coaching conversation. You notice that the treasurer stiffens and shuts down. Although you thought nothing of it, the treasurer feels like you violated a boundary and the "Vegas" rule for what was dis-cussed during the coaching conversation. Another rule of thumb that you can practice is to remember that when the conversation is over, it's over. The person you coached owns whatever they discussed and came up with, and it is theirs only to share.

One important exception to respecting confidentiality arises if sensitive or risky information is shared with you. In that conversation with the PTO treasurer, if the treasurer indicated that they planned to hurt themselves or someone else, you have a moral obligation to do something with that infor-mation. In organizations, HR professionals often refer to this as being "on notice." If an HR business partner is coaching a leader who has been having a tough time personally and that leader shares they have been thinking sui-cidal thoughts or considering taking extreme actions to harm others, the HR business partner must notify the appropriate authorities or designated indi-viduals within the organization. Information that could spare others from harm does not fall within the bounds of respecting confidentiality. In less extreme situations, you may also discover that the person you are coaching needs support that you are not equipped to provide – such as working with a therapist or social worker, a professional coach, or an employee relations colleague. If a situation like this arises, your responsibility is not to tell that person what they should do, but to help them become aware of and navigate their options. Ultimately, they own what they choose to do, and you can be of service to them and help them figure out what additional support they need.

Approaching social systems with a coaching mindset

In Chapter 6, we discussed ways a coaching mindset can influence how we think about and design organizations, including culture, climate, and people practices. The same could be said for our societal systems and structures. For example, we made the distinction between coercive and enabling systems. These are not restricted to companies. Instead, they reflect systems of control of any kind. Coercive control systems use formal policies, procedures, rules, and extrinsic punishments and rewards to motivate behavior. Enabling control systems instead rely more on social, psychological, and cultural influences and intrinsic motivation, giving the individual more autonomy.[14] A coaching mindset would favor an enabling approach. It would assume that people universally want to learn, grow, achieve mastery, be connected to others, and serve a higher purpose. It assumes that each person is in the best position to make decisions for themselves that align with those needs. Finally, it assumes that growth and change are most likely to occur when they align with the individual's goals and interests. Let's take a few examples of how this might apply to how we design a few of our core social systems.

It's easy to assume we all know the purpose of an educational system and how it should be designed, but approaches to education vary across countries, states, and institutions, and they can shift over time. As an example, in 2015, Governor Scott Walker attempted to change the University of Wisconsin's mission from searching for truth and improving the human condition to meeting the state's workforce needs. Many have called for radical education reform.[15] These calls are in response to increased understanding of how people learn and the reality that there's a need to equip students to move beyond mastering what is already known to acquiring the skills that help them discover new knowledge and tackle new problems. This reflects a significant shift in the role of educators and students and new approaches for learning. Drawing on our earlier metaphor, it suggests that teachers aren't just responsible for feeding the students a fish for a day, they must teach them how to fish. The American Psychological Association (APA)[16] has published the research base for learner-centered psychological principles that they argue should be considered in educational reform. This includes, among other things, creating more opportunity for choice; connecting learning to what is motivating for the learner; and embedding practice and reflection. Thus, there are strong parallels to the types of practices that make for effective coaching.

Marva Collins was an educator known for her open and loving approach to education.[17] She worked with students who were considered "unteachable" because of behavior challenges or presumed learning disabilities. Most of these students were low-income and overlooked by the public school system. Marva Collins's approach to educating was not unlike a coaching approach: she saw the students as capable and resourceful. She left behind assumptions and beliefs that had previously pigeonholed the students as troublesome. She brought an attitude of love and care to the students and leveraged tools like the Socratic method of asking questions to fully engage all students in classroom discussions. She challenged students to read complex literature and to think deeply about the stories and meaning through thought-provoking questions. She supported students in developing constructive mindsets and beliefs about themselves – that they were capable and attending school for their own learning, not simply because their parents or society said they had to. Her approach to education resulted in "problem students" turning into passionate readers and learners. Students who were thought to be illiterate learned to read and participate actively in class discussions. Students who may have otherwise been written off went on to pursue careers in law, medicine, business, and education.[18]

Taking inspiration from Marva Collins, we can approach education from the belief that students are creative, resourceful, and whole. We can bring curiosity, openness, and non-judgment to understand their challenges, interests, and what motivates and inspires them. In addition to students, coaching has been shown to be a powerful tool for teacher development. Peer coaching has been shown to boost teachers' performance – such as learning and successfully applying new teaching techniques or content – and also to reduce their feelings of isolation.[19] In one study, a formal coaching program supported teachers in learning and using a new intervention with students who had specific behavioral needs.[20] Peer-coaching programs for teachers can draw on the traditional coaching skill set of asking questions, listening, and noticing, and may also include direct forms of communication, like sharing feedback. In a coaching context, sharing feedback can also resemble noticing or "holding up the mirror." For instance, if Sando, a middle school teacher, is observing her peer Byron at the front of the classroom, their subsequent coaching conversation may include statements from Sando like, "Byron, I noticed that you called each student by name when you addressed them and the students perked up when they heard their names" or

"Byron, I noticed that when a student interrupted you to ask a question you reacted in a way that seemed irritated or annoyed." In both examples, Sando is "holding up the mirror" to Byron with her noticing and naming of his behavior. She can also follow these observations with a question, such as, "What bothered you about the student's question?"

Justice reform, too, may include moving from traditionally coercive approaches to more enabling. Take prison systems, for example. Rather than focusing on punishing and containing prisoners, Norway's prison system has adopted a "restorative justice" approach that focuses on rehabilitating prisoners and supporting whole-person growth.[21] Prisoners have opportunities to learn new skills and develop themselves through classes and programs that target both the mind and the body. As a result of this reform, Norway's recidivism rate has dropped from 60–70% to only 20%.[22] Prisoners are more likely to be employed once they are released, and Norway has even experienced economic benefits like reduced unemployment and a growing workforce. Contrast this with the United States, where research has shown that incarceration leads to higher rates of unemployment, recidivism, and reliance on public assistance.[23] Prison programs that focus on social and behavioral growth and skill building have been linked to lower rates of recidivism, including in the United States.[24] So how does this relate to coaching mindset and skills? This is an example of systemic change that requires a significant shift in attitudes and beliefs about criminals. It requires a belief that even criminals are whole people with potential to grow and change, who can complete their sentence and re-enter society with useful and productive skills and capabilities. Of course, there are extenuating circumstances that involve mental illness, substance abuse, and other challenges. Our intent here is not to oversimplify criminal justice, but to highlight shifts that can benefit not only prisoners, but economies and societies where they live and work.

Research has also shown that policing can be improved through more enabling communication approaches. A University of San Diego class on policing suggests that the most effective policing occurs when officers listen 80% of the time and talk 20% of the time[25] (by the way, that's a rough metric we share with our students about how coaches engage with clients, too). The course on effective police communication focuses on noticing and being mindful of their own body language, asking simple open-ended questions one at a time (not unlike coaching, some of the best questions are five to six words and never "stacked" – one question at a time!), and understanding how emotional contagion works and could affect the officer or people they are communicating with. More enabling communication (listening, asking questions, being curious) has been shown to lead to de-escalation in police situations.[26] Letting go of assumptions and practicing active listening equips officers to better understand a situation and exercise clear judgment, rather than reacting from a place of fear or bias. Randomized control studies have also demonstrated positive impacts of mindfulness practices on police officers stress and quality of life[27] and de-escalation, positively impacting the communities they serve.[28]

Coaching as a tool for transformational change

Read any newspaper and you will see that the world is facing an array of daunting and pervasive challenges including racism, sexism, political polarization, climate change, and threats to democracy, to name a few. Significant and transformational change will be required to resolve big, complex challenges like these. Transformational change cannot happen without fundamental shifts in mindsets, behaviors, and culture. This is one of the reasons that these challenges are so pervasive. Change is stressful because it creates fear and uncertainty. When people go through change, their optimism drops by 6% and they show a 19% drop in stress management skills compared to those not experiencing change.[29] Change can threaten our sense of security, who we are, and what we value. We may fear personal loss as a part of that change. To change, people need to feel safe and to be given opportunities to learn, practice, and ultimately enact changes in everyday actions. Inertia is strong because it requires less effort than change and is far less threatening.

Shifting mindsets and behaviors is often much harder than we expect because it requires ongoing attention, self-control, and motivation. One reason the challenges above are so pervasive is because they are complex problems that will take years or decades to resolve, inevitably facing setbacks. Resilience is critical in helping people navigate the often-jagged path to a new behavioral norm. Furthermore, resistance to change, us-versus-them thinking, or righteous feelings about the old way or the "good old days" leave people stuck in what was versus being open to what could be. People need to develop awareness, align to purpose, and build their cognitive agility to be able to consider multiple perspectives and ways forward. For people to change, they need to be comfortable identifying when negative emotions around the change are surfacing and learn the skills to manage these fears appropriately. Successful regulation of emotions also involves learning to shift one's lens to elicit more positive feelings. Also, think back to our "research spotlight" in Chapter 4, where Dr. Angela Passarelli shared the power of coaching around possibility. When we ask big, bold questions about what is possible in the future, we not only dream up new possibilities, we also activate positive emotional centers of our brain.

A growing body of research[30] indicates that coaching has positive effects on the resilience of managers during transformation efforts. As an example, Anthony Grant and colleagues conducted a randomized controlled study in which nursing sector senior managers and executives attended a half-day leadership training and either received coaching or were included in a waitlist control group (where they received coaching at a later time). The researchers administered a set of assessments, including goal attainment, resilience, well-being, and others. The results showed that coaching was associated with a significant improvement in goal attainment, resilience, and well-being over the control group. This is important because transformations take years to plan, implement, and sustain, requiring continued energy from managers even in the face of resistance and setbacks. As an example, combating systemic racism through diversity, inclusion, and belonging initiatives can unfortunately trigger a sense of identity threat and stress. Becoming more inclusive starts with identifying and understanding where you are in your own journey, clarifying why it's important, and understanding your role in a complex social system and the strategies and behaviors you can employ to foster inclusion. This journey can be very uncomfortable, meaning that building resilience in the face of deep-rooted identity threats for majority group members can help remove barriers to exploring biases. BetterUp research[31] found that when leader resilience is improved through coaching, the rate of inclusive leadership behaviors also increases. Resilient leaders are more likely to engage in inclusive leadership behaviors, such as creating environments of psychological safety and equally inviting participation, encouraging all team members to meaningfully contribute and participate. Teams with highly resilient leaders have higher resilience, and also report a higher sense of belonging.

The challenges our society is wrestling with are complex and will require collective commitment and individual shifts in mindsets and behaviors. Coaching can help each of us to make that journey and to help others along the way. The good news is that there is likely to be a tipping point. Researchers at the University of Pennsylvania[32] designed a series of experiments within online social communities, manipulating the population size of the communities and the size of the minority groups working to change an established belief. What they observed was remarkably consistent across experimental conditions – widespread change could be achieved rapidly once 25% of the population advocated for the change. Getting to 25% feels much more achievable than 100% and if we each show up a little more coach-like, we might be able to get there even sooner. Research has also shown that mindfulness is a powerful tool for changing attitudes and behaviors related to climate change.[33] Two separate studies found that mindfulness was key to helping people become more aware of climate risks and also adopting new personal behaviors that have a positive impact on the environment.[34] Individuals who participated in a mindfulness program related to climate and environment changed behaviors in areas of their life that included transportation habits, diet, household energy use, and more. Bottom-up change starts with the behavior of individuals. When growing numbers of individuals change their behavior in support of a big goal, meaningful shifts begin to occur. Transformational change engages both the minds and hearts of individuals,[35] requiring shifts in attitudes, beliefs, and behaviors in support of a bigger goal.

Parting thoughts

In this book we have explored the mindsets and skills that coaches leverage to support others' growth and self-discovery. Along the way, we shared how adopting a coaching mindset and applying coaching skills in an array of situations can open up relationships, communication, others' potential, and what we believe to be possible. We fervently believe that leveraging a coaching mindset and skill set can shift the way you understand yourself, others, and the world, and how you show up and impact those situations. Perhaps we sound overly optimistic in our beliefs about what is possible. Imagine for a moment what could be possible if everyone let go of judgment, the need to be right, relying on assumptions and jumping to conclusions. Think of a few people in your life. What would change if each of them picked up these practices, even if only 50% of the time?

From here, we hope that you will go out into the world and experiment with what you have learned in this book. You may not figure it out or nail your coaching questions right away – that's all part of the learning process. Use the cycle of behavior change that you learned in Chapter 3 to create a process for trying something new (asking questions, turning on your curiosity, listening at level 2 or 3), get feedback on how that behavior landed, reflect on how you did and what you noticed, and decide what you'll try again or instead next time.

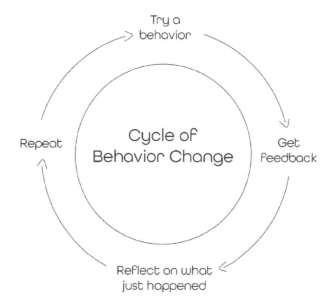

Of course, we can't close the book without one final reflection. Take a moment to pause and think about what you learned in this book. Use the questions below to support your reflection.

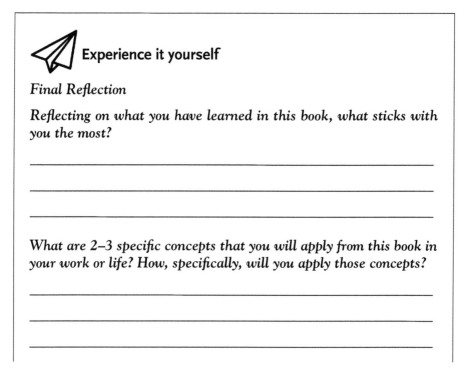

Experience it yourself

Final Reflection

Reflecting on what you have learned in this book, what sticks with you the most?

_____

_____

_____

What are 2–3 specific concepts that you will apply from this book in your work or life? How, specifically, will you apply those concepts?

_____

_____

_____

What questions still remain for you after reading this book?

_____

_____

_____

Who else would benefit from reading this book, and why?

_____

_____

_____

Chapter 7 Key idea

Applying a coaching mindset and coaching skills in your day-to-day can make you more effective in a range of situations – even in navigating those conversations about politics with relatives at the holiday dinner table. At scale, a coaching mindset can create a better world.

Want to learn more? Check out

Smiling Mind provides a library of guided meditations and mindfulness exercises. Visit https://www.smilingmind.com.au/ to learn more
Get daily inspiration, ideas, and resources from www.mindful.org/

Recommended reading

50 ways coaches can change the world by C.J. Hayden

A curious mind: the secret to a bigger life by Brian Grazer and Charles Fishman

Marva Collins' way by Marva Collins and Civia Tamarkin

Notes

1 Stanier, M. B. (2016). *The coaching habit: Say less, ask more & change the way you lead forever*. Toronto CA: Box of Crayons Press.

2 Stanier, M. B. (2020). *The advice trap: Be humble, stay curious & change the way you lead forever*. Box of Crayons Press, based in Toronto ON CA.

3 Flaherty, J. (2010). *Coaching* (3rd ed.). Routledge. https://doi.org/10.4324/9780080964294

4 Passmore, J., & Marianetti, O. (2007). The role of mindfulness in coaching. *The Coaching Psychologist, 3*(3), 131–137.

5 Manhart, K. (2004). The limits of multitasking. *Scientific American Mind, 14*(5), 62–67.

6 Harris, J. III, & Lewis, T. (1986). Human [Recorded by The Human League]. On *Crash* [Album]. A&M, Virgin.

7 Gino, F. (2018, September–October). The business case for curiosity. *Harvard Business Review*. https://hbr.org/2018/09/the-business-case-for-curiosity

8 Silvia, P. J., & Kashdan, T. B. (2009). Interesting things and curious people: Exploration and engagement as transient states and enduring strengths. *Social and Personality Psychology Compass, 3*(5), 785–797. https://doi.org/10.1111/j.1751-9004.2009.00210.x

9 Lurie, Z. (2019, January–February). SurveyMonkey's CEO on creating a culture of curiosity. *Harvard Business Review*. https://hbr.org/2019/01/surveymonkeys-ceo-on-creating-a-culture-of-curiosity

10 Gino. (2018). Business case for curiosity.

11 McCarthy, K. (2021, May 17). School bus driver says kindergartners' curiosity helped stop armed hijacking. *ABC News*. https://abcnews.go.com/GMA/Living/school-bus-driver-kindergartners-curiosity-helped-stop-armed/story?id=77732521

12 Voss, C., & Raz, T. (2016). *Never split the difference: Negotiating as if your life depended on it*. Harper Collins - New York.

13 Gregory, J. B., & Levy, P. E. (2011). It's not me, it's you: A multilevel examination of variables that impact employee coaching relationships. *Consulting Psychology Journal: Practice and Research, 63*(2), 67–88. https://doi.org/10.1037/a0024152

14 Carenys, J. (2012). Management control systems: A historical perspective. *International Journal of Economy, Management and Social Sciences, 1*(1), 1–18.

15 Blinkoff, E., Hirsh-Pasek, K., & Hadani, H. S. (2020, November 12). An unprecedented time in education demands unprecedented change. *Brookings*. www.brookings.edu/blog/education-plus-development/2020/11/13/an-unprecedented-time-in-education-demands-unprecedented-change/

16 Alexander, P. A., & Murphy, P. K. (1998). The research base for APA's learner-centered psychological principles. In N. M. Lambert & B. L. McCombs (Eds.), *How students learn: Reforming schools through learner-centered education* (pp. 25–60). American Psychological Association. https://doi.org/10.1037/10258-001

17 Collins, M., & Tamarkin, C. (1990). *Marva Collins' way*, New York. Jeremy P. Tarcher, Inc.

18 Biondi, C. A. (2018, August 20). Marva Collins, her method, and her 'philosophy for living'. *The Objective Standard*. https://theobjectivestandard.com/2018/08/marva-collins-her-method-and-her-philosophy-for-living/

19 Slater, C. L., & Simmons, D. L. (2001). The design and implementation of a peer coaching program. *American Secondary Education, 29*(3) 67–76.

20 Stormont, M., Reinke, W. M., Newcomer, L., Marchese, D., & Lewis, C. (2015). Coaching teachers' use of social behavior interventions to improve children's outcomes: A review of the literature. *Journal of Positive Behavior Interventions, 17*(2), 69–82. https://doi.org/10.1177/1098300714550657

21 Dorisuren, B. (2020, November 2020). Norway's prison system benefits its economy. *The Borgen Project.* https://borgenproject.org/norways-prison-system/

22 Sterbenz, C. (2014, December 11). Why Norway's prison system is so successful. *Business Insider.* www.businessinsider.com/why-norways-prison-system-is-so-successful-2014-12

23 Mueller-Smith, M. (2015). The criminal and labor market impacts of incarceration. *Unpublished Working Paper,* 1–18.

24 Andrews, D. A., & Bonta, J. (2003). *The psychology of criminal conduct* (3rd ed.). Cincinnati, OH: Anderson.

25 Fritsvold, E. (n.d.). Police communication skills matter more than ever: Here's why. *University of San Diego Online.* https://onlinedegrees.sandiego.edu/police-communication-important-today/

26 Crisis Prevention Institute. (2019, March 20). *Verbal de-escalation training for police.* www.crisisprevention.com/Library/De-Escalation-Training-for-Police

27 Trombka, M., Demarzo, M., Campos, D., Antonio, S. B., Cicuto, K., Walcher, A. L., Garcia-Campayo, J., Schuman-Olivier, Z., & Rocha, N. S. (2021). Mindfulness training improves quality of life and reduces depression and anxiety symptoms among police officers: Results From the POLICE study – A multicenter randomized controlled trial. *Frontiers in Psychiatry, 12,* 624876. https://doi.org/10.3389/fpsyt.2021.624876

28 Suttie, J. (2016, May 18). How mindfulness is changing law enforcement. *Greater Good Magazine.* https://greatergood.berkeley.edu/article/item/how_mindfulness_is_changing_law_enforcement

29 BetterUp. (2020). *BetterUp member data.* San Fransisco, CA: BetterUp Unpublished Member Data.

30 Grant, A. M., Curtayne, L., & Burton, G. (2009). Executive coaching enhances goal attainment, resilience and workplace well-being: A randomised controlled study. *The Journal of Positive Psychology, 4*(5), 396–407. https://doi.org/10.1080/17439760902992456

   Sherlock-Storey, M., Moss, M., & Timson, S. (2013). Brief coaching for resilience during organisational change – An exploratory study. *The Coaching Psychologist, 9*(1), 19–26.

   Timson, S. (2015). Exploring what clients find helpful in a brief resilience coaching programme: A qualitative study. *The Coaching Psychologist, 11*(2), 81–88.

31 Jeannotte, A., Eatough, E., & Kellerman, G. R. (2020). Resilience in an age of uncertainty: Cultivating resilient leaders, teams, and organizations. *BetterUp* [Report]. https://grow.betterup.com/resilience

32 Sloane, J. (2018, June 7). Research finds tipping point for large-scale social change. *University of Pennsylvania, Annenberg School for Communication*. www.asc.upenn.edu/news-events/news/research-finds-tipping-point-large-scale-social-change

33 Wamsler, C. (2018). Mind the gap: The role of mindfulness in adapting to increasing risk and climate change. *Sustainability Science, 13*(4), 1121–1135. https://doi.org/10.1007/s11625-017-0524-3

34 Wamsler. (2018). Mind the gap, 1121–1135.
   Grabow, M., Bryan, T., Checovich, M. M., Converse, A. K., Middlecamp, C., Mooney, M., Torres, E. R., Younkin, S. G., & Barrett, B. (2018). Mindfulness and climate change action: A feasibility study. *Sustainability, 10*(5), 1508–1532. https://doi.org/10.3390/su10051508

35 Gass, R. (2010). What is transformational change. In *Framing deep change: Essays on transformative social change* (pp. 12–14). Berkeley, CA: Center for Transformative Change.

Appendix
Tools and activities to further your learning

As we described in Chapter 3, learning and change are facilitated through active processing, practice, and reflection. Coaches use a wide range of tools to support that process – many of which we've embedded throughout the book. In case you're interested in furthering your own learning or expanding your repertoire of tools you can share with others, we've included a few more of our favorites for you to use.

Self-observation exercises

Observe yourself in the act of asking questions in the various areas of your life, such as professional situations, family relationships, social interactions, etc.

- Notice, without judging. Be curious about what you notice.
- Keep a log (in your journal) of what you observe in at least 3–5 conversations each day.
- Do this self-observation for one week.
- At the end of the week, review the log of your observations – without judging.

Without judgment, notice how your emotional states impact others and how others' emotional states impact you.

You might discover yourself thinking something like, "Oh, that's interesting! I never noticed that. Wow, look at what happens to X when I am feeling _____." For example, you might notice that you always greet one of your students with big smiles and warm welcomes, and that you feel really happy when you see him. You might then notice, "Wow, after I greet him that way, I see his face relax, his smile widens, and he calmly sits at his desk." Or you might notice that when you were feeling tired and anxious and you curtly asked the school secretary for a form, that her shoulders hunched up and she was snappy in return. As you do this noticing, try again to refrain from self-criticism. Just notice. Name. Observe. Journal.

Call a friend to catch up as you normally would. Listen for and notice assessments that you make – about yourself, others, your job, whatever else

- What's at the core of these assessments?
- What assertions (facts) underlie them?

Use your journal to capture your reflections

Journal prompts

What is your story, up until now? How does that story align with the story of you as your best self?

In a public place, sit and observe, working on level 3 listening (Chapter 4).

- What do you notice about how people are feeling?
- The energy in the room?
- What can you notice with your eyes closed?

Record your reflections in your journal. What data do you have access to when you listen in this way? How might you incorporate this into your life and relationships?

A few questions for the road as you finish this book . . .

- How will you be different?
- What will you now notice?
- How will you share what you now know?
- How do you want to show up – at work, at home, at large?
- What's next? What support will you need?
- What will you take from this book? Was it what you expected?
- What will you remember?

Behavioral practices

Focus on seeing your own life and experience through fresh eyes

- Assume the identity of someone else you admire and experience your day-to-day life through their eyes. This could be someone you know or another figure, like Yoda, Jesus, a political figure, a celebrity, a role model, etc.

- Notice when you are making an assessment or telling a story that doesn't serve you. See if you can write a new one that leaves you feeling better or more empowered.

Use your journal to capture your observations

Try a visioning exercise to envision achievement of your goals or changes you want to bring to your life.

- Pick a challenge or goal that is top of mind for you now.
- Imagine it's six months from now (or three months, a year – you can choose the appropriate time frame).
- Imagine that you have achieved that goal or overcome that challenge.
- Paint a very specific picture in your mind. What does it look like, feel like? What are you doing, where are you? Who are you with? What happened when you achieved the goal or completed the challenge?
- If helpful, you can give yourself permission to think unconstrained. Don't worry about the "what ifs" or obstacles that might have arisen on your way to achieving this goal. Assume everything worked out wonderfully as you create your vision.
- Revisit your vision often. Use this to pull your behavior toward the outcome that you want.
- If helpful, you can also work backward from that vision – what happened in the months leading up to your success that made it a reality? This can help you identify specific steps or milestones along the way. Celebrate those little victories and milestones as you go!

Topic specific exercises

Listening

- Pick five people from different parts of your life (family, friends, colleagues, etc.).
- In a normal conversation with them, listen for the assessments (stories) and assertions (facts) they share.
- If you could give them totally candid feedback, what would you say about their stories and assessments? What patterns or connections do you see? Where are their stories coming from?
- Note your observations in your journal.

Perspective

(1) Read the book *Zoom* by Istvan Banyai and/or watch the animated video on YouTube (www.youtube.com/watch?v=JMhUujrN4iU).
(2) Reflect. Respond to the following prompts in your journal:
    (a) What stood out to you?
    (b) What are the benefits of "Zooming in"?
    (c) What do you gain by "Zooming out"? What do you lose?
    (d) How have you seen this play out in organizations? What are the positive and negative consequences of close-in or far-out thinking and management?
    (e) How does this apply to coaching?

Mindfulness exercises

There are many ways to practice mindfulness. In our class, we encourage our students to experiment with a variety of exercises to learn what works best for them.

- Centering exercises
  Often centering exercises use breathing to help you regain or maintain your composure and remind yourself that you are safe and in balance. One type of breathing exercise we introduce in class is called *box breathing*. This is a simple technique used by the Navy SEALs and involves the following steps:
  1. Inhale for 4 seconds
  2. Hold the air in your lungs for 4 seconds
  3. Exhale for 4 seconds
  4. Hold your lungs empty for 4 seconds

- Meditations
  Meditation is a practice of clearing your mind and focusing your attention. There are many forms of meditation including walking, breathing, sitting, eating, resting, and so on. Two meditations we introduce in the class are a body scan and mindful eating.
  To do a body scan, sit in a chair or lie on the floor.
- Start from your head or your toes, giving this starting point your full attention. If you start with your toes, notice your toes – become aware of them, how do they feel? You can even wiggle them a little, or feel the ground under them if you are sitting.

- Work your way up or down your body, depending on where you began, giving each part of your body your full attention. If you started with the top of your head, focus next on your forehead, then your eyebrows, then your eyes, and so on.
- At each part of your body, what do you notice? Give each stop along your body the same amount of deliberate attention.
- If you want to weave in gratitude, you can feel gratitude for your health or for certain parts of your body as you go (e.g., thank you, heart for your steady beat; thank you, legs for getting me around each day)
- Once you reach the other end of your body, notice how you feel.

To try a mindful eating exercise yourself, follow these steps:

1. Select a snack or piece of food (e.g., an orange slice).
2. Approach the food with a beginner's mindset, as if you've never seen it before. First, look at it from all angles. Notice the color, shape, texture. Feel it – notice its temperature, texture, and consistency.
3. Imagine the path that the food took to arrive in your hand. Who had to touch it, how it was transported, the many lives involved in enabling it to nourish you.
4. Smell the food.
5. Begin to taste it, but do so very slowly. Feel the weight on your tongue, the textures in your mouth, the flavor and how your body responds. Hold it in your mouth for a minute before you begin to chew.
6. As you chew, do so slowly. See if you can chew each bite 30 times while staying very present to the experience of eating this way.

- Poetry
  Reading poetry with full attention and without judgment is another way to practice mindfulness. Again, we encourage you to try different styles and authors to find something that speaks to you. One author whom we enjoy and introduce in class is the Irish poet and philosopher John O'Donohue. We begin our class with his poem titled "A New Beginning."
- Music
  Listening to music can be a powerful way to help you shift your mind from worrying to a more focused and relaxed state. You can do this with any type of music, and you can also find specific meditation music if you want to try that. The goal of the practice is to "be." Follow these steps:

1. Choose a song that you enjoy listening to.
2. Get into a comfortable position.

3. Focus on the music. If you find yourself thinking about other things, redirect your attention to the present moment (without judgment), the sound of the music, and the feelings in your body that the music evokes. Try to really feel the music.

Still looking for more resources? Check out what the organizations below have to offer!

The Mayo Clinic mindfulness site (mayoclinic.org/healthy-lifestyle/ consumer-health/in-depth/mindfulness-exercises)
Mindful (mindful.org/)
Meditation Oasis (meditationoasis.com/)
Plum Village (plumvillage.org)
Positive Psychology (positivepsychology.com/)

Index

Note: Page numbers in *italics* indicate a figure, page numbers in **bold** indicate a table, and page numbers followed by an "n" indicate a note on the corresponding page.

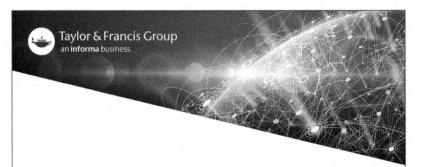